HAUNTED PLACES
OF WESTERN NEW YORK
A SUPERNATURAL TOUR GUIDE

BY MASON WINFIELD

WITH:

MICHAEL BASTINE

FRANKLIN LAVOIE

AMY REED

MAP BY KENNETH SHERIDAN
DIGITAL IMAGING BY CHRISTOPHER JANIGA

© 2003 Western New York Wares Inc.
All rights reserved
Printed by Petit Printing

Address all inquiries to:

Brian Meyer, Publisher
Western New York Wares Inc.
P.O. Box 733
Ellicott Station
Buffalo, NY 14205
e-mail: buffalobooks@att.net
Web site: www.buffalobooks.com

This book was published and printed in Buffalo, NY
ISBN: 1-879201-45-3

Visit our Internet site:
www.buffalobooks.com

PUBLISHER'S PONDERINGS

Connoisseurs of classic films may remember the cinematic moment. In the final lines of *The Ghost and Mrs. Muir*, Rex Harrison welcomes Gene Tierney to the spirit world. "And now you will never be tired again. Come, Lucia. Come, my dear."

I saw the movie as a kid. I didn't grasp all its nuances, but I did understand early in life that the paranormal doesn't have to be a bone-chilling topic. As I mentioned in my introduction to Mason Winfield's first book – *Shadows of the Western Door* – six years ago, my mom deserves the credit for instilling in me a respect for things of the spirit realm. She was a deeply spiritual woman, despite the fact that she lived most of her life not associated with any organized religion. She believed in the after-life. She believed in spirit visitations. She was convinced that our departed loved ones watched over us.

Against that backdrop, one can understand why I have special affinity for Mason's fine line of books. *Shadows*, *A Ghosthunter's Journal* and *Spirits of the Great Hill* have created one of the most successful "franchises" in our small but growing regional publishing company.

As I've said so many times before, no publishing odyssey is a one-person endeavor. My thanks to Michele Ratzel, our business manager and a wonderful friend who has played a defining role in our entrepreneurial adventures for a dozen years. I also thank Tom Connolly, who does a stellar job in overseeing our distribution and marketing efforts. The crew at Petit Printing also deserves credit. But without Mason's passion for research and flair for writing, I wouldn't be penning this introduction. Mason, here's hoping we'll hit a dozen titles by 2015!

My mom passed away a month after we finalized plans to publish this book. It was a bittersweet passage. She had been suffering from many health ailments for quite some time. And she missed my dad more than words can convey. Her husband of 53 years – and her best friend -- died in August of 2000.

Maybe it's my over-active imagination. Or maybe it's just Mason's contagious enthusiasm. But if I close my eyes, I can almost hear my dad's tender voice as he reaches out to mom. "And now you will never be tired again. Come, Jean. Come my dear."

Brian Meyer, Publisher
August, 2003

INTRODUCTION

I

Life itself is a wonder, and every spot on earth has mystery. Some spots have more than others, and that's what this book is about, a tour guide to mystery-places in Western New York, the traditional Seneca territory. The first big chunk of this book addresses hauntings, in themes: haunted inns, churches, battlefields... Following is a study of sacred sites and movements, Native American and Euroamerican. The last chapter is the edgiest, a profile of natural energy-points and "X-Zones" of general weirdness.

Some of these tours are direct, but the courses of others may confound readers. Rather than use weaker sites to get shapelier routes, I went where the good sites were. People expecting another *Shadows of the Western Door* should enjoy this book's different pace and focus. It's a tour guide. In *Shadows* and *Spirits of the Great Hill* you read about sites. Take this one with you and experience them. Or let it take you.

This study of hauntings is limited. If a haunted something didn't fit into one of the categories I picked, I had nothing to say about it. And if it's a phenomenon and not a site, there's nothing to tour. I also wanted to pick public sites and already-published material. I didn't want to "break" a ghost story about *your* house.

Some material in this book is taken from *Shadows* and *Spirits*. Of course. It's a tour guide. You can't leave famous sites out. But I'd do something else before I wrote a recycled book. There's as much new material here as in a complete book like *Shadows*, but it's more compressed. And some of the material in "HTG" as we call it is as exciting as any I've ever put together. Waking people up to the history under them is part of my mission in Western New York. Showing them sacred and visionary sites is part of my debt to the world. Some of these haven't been recognized in a hundred years. Now if we can get them preserved so everyone can visit them...

A word or two about ghosts. I think ghosts exist, at least at the moment they appear, but I don't know why they happen or what they are. Several patterns go with hauntings in the popular imagination, and I mention them when they come up, but I don't want to seem to "explain" a ghost. The closest I get to anything like that is when I think of sites, buildings or areas that get a lot of talk. There may be some reason, possibly connected to "energy" that can't be documented, but that may show itself in the simple outbreak of folklore. Of course, to many world societies the idea of this life-force wasn't radical. It's *ch'i* to the Asians, *kaa* to the old

Egyptians, *orenda* to the Iroquois.

I use the term "spooks" to refer to psychic activity. I do it to save time. I don't imply that I think demons or the spirits of dead people are behind the effects witnesses often describe, but figuring out what is isn't the job I've set myself, nor did I try to decide whether this or that UFO/Bigfoot report was valid. Taking people on hundreds of journeys as a writer has been more interesting to me than trying to validate a handful of cases as an investigator. I doubt I'll ever change. This book has to be considered a collection of folklore, a guide to places at which supernatural traditions gather.

I don't think you'll see a ghost if you take these tours. A ghost is a performing art like a dance, not a steady one like a statue. There's only a tiny possibility that a paranormal-psychic event will replay itself at the time you're on hand. At least with this book you'll know the place. And for me, the place has always been the thing. I think of ghosts as almost forces of nature, and places that host them as "energy" sites. The sites themselves are vision-places.

Many people helped this book, but several were co-authors. Algonquin teacher and activist Michael Bastine opened a door for me into Native American spirituality. My words are his wisdom. Artist and mystic Franklin LaVoie is the pioneer student of the ancient patterns of Western New York: astronomy, geometry, mythology, tradition... He's helped me for years, asking nothing back. His insights shape my every understanding of earthly sites and regional tradition. Amy Reed is a *feng-shui* consultant and a student of old spirituality. Her general savvy and stick-to-it-iveness have helped this book in every way. These were my confidants, putting up with my pestering to get some basic idea straight.

Here's a special thanks to my late friend Rodger Sweetland of East Aurora. Like Sheldon Fisher of Fishers and David Robinson of Swain, he was the spirit of the independent Yankee scholar. I'm flattered to be someone he thought of as "all right." Too quietly he left us. When we meet again in that speculators' Valhalla, he can update me on all the questions we shared: Where are Red Jacket's bones and the Senecas' Great Hill? Who set the Circle-henge and the Bluff Point stones? Who were the last Atlanteans, the first Americans?

East Aurora, NY
August, 2003

CONTENTS

Part I - A TOUR OF HAUNTS

1) Haunted Inns   Page   8
2) Haunted Mansions   Page 17
3) College Spirit   Page 26
4) Grave Haunts   Page 31
5) Holy Spirits   Page 37
6) Battlefield Haunts   Page 43
7) Haunted Highways   Page 53
8) Haunted Theaters   Page 59
9) Haunted Landmarks   Page 66
10) Spooky Communities Page 75

Part II - WAYS of the SPIRIT

A) Vision-Places   Page 84
B) Along Spirit Way   Page 91

Part III - The X-PLACES

A) The X-Zones   Page 105
B) The Power Points   Page 112

for Frances Elizabeth Ward Winfield,
who passed into spirit January 15, 2003

A Southern lady.

"THE GHOSTS WALK," DIGITAL IMAGE BY TIM BAILEY AND CHRISTOPHER JANIGA (5-G PRESS)

1
Haunted Inns

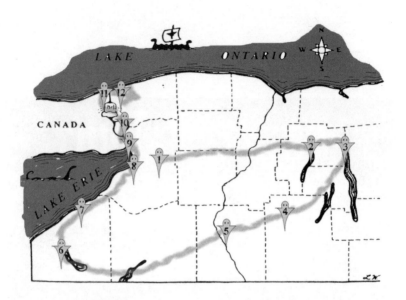

Let's start with something we could hardly have left out, "the haunted inn." How many centuries - millennia - has it appeared in literature? What a theme it is in film. Take a little tour with us of Western New York's haunted inns. Not all of them are still-functioning inns, but that shouldn't worry you. You can still visit for dinner and drinks, and have one with the spirits in each stop. Let's start at a significant corner.

1) The historic Big Tree Road - Route 20A - opened the Holland Purchase to settlement. Where it meets the ancient north-south trail that became Olean Road is a charming wooden structure that opened in 1820 as a sort of general store. It was quickly discovered that **East Aurora** could accommodate an almost unlimited number of saloons, and today's Tony Rome's **Globe Hotel** has been a drinkery in some form or other since. Today's Globe is family-friendly, but tales about the town's early history make it sound like a wild west show. They say a couple guys got into a shootout with what would have to have been flintlocks in the 1830s when one of them stepped off a carriage. The loser staggered into the front door of the Globe and expired on the landing, which (under the current flooring) still shows bloodstains.

A Tour of Haunts

~ ~ ~ 9 ~ ~ ~

This tale is very hard to confirm or deny; but no wonder there may be ghosts here. In 1867 the third floor was added as a dance hall, and today the top two floors hold offices and apartments. There have been a couple of deaths up here, but none of them were violent or mysterious. People just went to bed and "woke up dead" as my kid-friends would say. Most of the random psychic activity happens on the top two floors. Workmen find their tools misplaced over night. Sounds and electrical effects are proverbial among the staff. After a former owner they nickname their regular apparition "Old Vic," usually spotted in the bar area. Many living East Aurorans knew Old Vic in life, but few recall that near the end of his years he had a physical condition so prominent that it would have told in profile. New employees who say they've seen the tall, shadowy shape and fail to mention this feature get a beer-bath. June 2001 was a great month for ghost reports in East Aurora, and one of the most electrifying I've ever recorded comes from this period. (The image of "Old Vic" appeared to a regular patron at the Globe and seemed to be prophetic of... something you'll have to join the East Aurora ghost walk and make it to the end to hear.) Now shoot east on the historic Big Tree Road.

2) One Halloween the **Canandaigua** *Daily Messenger* did an ample piece about the ghosts at today's **Lincoln Hill Inn**. Well they should. It's a cheery place, but they may have their "extra" guests. The restaurant is converted from a farmhouse that had been with a single family for a hundred and six years, and spirits seem to sing when members of the Dewey clan are back to dine, visit, and marry. A branch of a nearby black walnut tree cracked like thunder, fell, and miraculously hung in place above the rock gardens at a Dewey wedding, as if some spontaneous, powerful presence in the place was paying them tribute, marking the start of the wedding with a dramatic gesture no one could miss. Some invisible imp acted up in the kitchen, lofting a lid off its container and landing it several feet away. People were convinced that someone was speaking to the family that had been here so long. Current owners Bill and Cheryl Ward had heard the stories, but their personal awakening came when they were doing some excavating and noticed many psychic occurrences, as if spirits stirred when the ground was disturbed. Some of the staff have stories of their own. Many complain of a creepy feeling when they close the upstairs alone. It has to

be the simple energy, the presence of spirit, to which they react. Some psychically gifted diners tell their server they feel spirits upstairs. With a twinkle, sometimes they offer to interpret, a proposition many servers decline.

3) In the mid-1800s they called it *Bellehurst* ("Beautiful forest"), and the name stuck to this piece of land over the lake with so much history near **Geneva**. Site of a Seneca village and home to the Council of the Six Nations, it became a long-range but short-term piece of Massachusetts and, by 1810, held the first glass company west of Albany. The builder of the first "modern" residence on it (the 1824 Hermitage) never lived in it, and it was rumored haunted almost from the start. A series of between-the-lines owners followed. (One blade embezzled funds from the Covent Garden Theater in London, married his stepmother, fled to the states under a new name, and is credited with the tunnel so persistent in folklore.) Mrs. Carrie Young Harron bought the land the day she saw it. Then she divorced her New York City husband, married dashing Captain Collins, her manager, and set fifty men to work on her mansion. Four years and 475K later, 48 men finished **Belhurst Castle** (1892). (One died when he fell from the tower and another went crazy on the roof.) In 1932 the castle opened as a speakeasy and casino and continued as a restaurant until 1975. By November 1992, Belhurst Castle was a four-diamond restaurant and inn listed on the National Register of Historic Places. Maybe it's also one of the most haunted. The sense of the romantic - in the artistic sense, meaning "fantastic and Gothic" - dominates the folklore, which includes hidden treasure, eloping lovers from exotic locales, a "beautiful Italian opera singer" killed in the likely-mythical tunnel, and handfuls of ghosts, including the "woman in white" seen on the lawn by dozens of guests.

4) Thrice-married farmer Samuel Fitch Woodworth built his 17-room Italianate villa in 1860. Now on the National Register of Historic Places, his **Cohocton** home may have been a stop on the Underground Railroad. (It held a trapdoor, crawlspace, and false basement.) Woodworth was descended of Walter Woodworth, prime ancestor of most American Woodworths, born in 1612 in Lancashire and landing in Massachusetts in 1631. Sam Woodworth's family came to the Finger Lakes in 1835. Family history may be significant, since the house seems steeped in Woodworth spirits. One of

A Tour of Haunts

Walter's six daughters (great-aunt of Sam Woodworth) was named Mehitabel, and she died not long after an accusation of witchcraft. (*Maybe* she was executed.) "She was probably a good witch," says Fran Ambroselli, owner of today's **Villa Serendip**, a thriving B&B. "This house is watched by good spirits." Among them are probably Sam Woodworth's three granddaughters who thought of turning the family home into a tea room. While not known to be haunted by any named apparition, there is something about the place. During the long and all-hours pro-am restoration of the neglected building, needed tools or supplies simply "appeared," falling out of open panels in the walls so often that it became proverbial. The spooks here are multisensory. One Civil War veteran of the Woodworth family seems to announce his return by whistling battle-hymns at berry-season. The baby that cries and coos is the most touching. One of Samuel Woodworth's daughters died at three months. She seems pleased to see all the guests.

5) Most of the early records of the town were lost in a fire, so there's a lot we won't know about **Angelica**, and that's sad, because there was a lot to know. Just after the Revolution the Genesee Valley started to hop, and many prominent Americans settled here, like Robert Morris, signer of the Declaration, who owned the land under today's **Angelica Inn**. Designed by Harvey Ellis, the 1883 Angelica Inn is atmospheric, an Arts & Crafts Movement home that, like others of that style, tends to collect ghosts. [Another of Ellis' homes, the Ashton House (Galveston, TX), is also reputedly haunted.] Previous owners told generic stories about "spirits" in the Inn, and over the years a handful of guests have been more specific. A man who lived in what became today's ballroom spent a night petrified by a silvery, shimmering presence in a doorway. People in the 1825 guest house complained of someone pounding up and down the stairs all one night, at times sounding like a small mob no one ever saw. Kids here sense the influences, and at night the Inn's dogs, both small and high-strung, won't go upstairs, destination of the mystery-footsteps. On several occasions some midnight phantom pounded on the front door. At other times music boxes played themselves in different rooms. Lights turned themselves on, once three times in an hour, even with the wall switch off. Owner Cynthia Petito had always presumed that things like this weren't possible, but she got her educa-

tion at the Angelica Inn. Maybe it's all related to the old gravestone behind the pond, too faded to read. Maybe it comes from the nearby mausoleum to which the owners of the Angelica Inn are traditional key-keepers. (No one's opened it since 1935.) Some spirit must be calling for articulation; but it's important to note that it's a good-natured one. No one's ever seriously bothered here. And the curiosities pile up. Cynthia Petito bought a piece of furniture to go with the Inn, and shortly after Rushford historian Homer Norton gave her a picture of a woman standing next to the very item.

6) Ghosts seem to gravitate to holy places, and people gravitate to special ones. The summer-seasoned **Chautauqua Institution** and its biggest and most distinctive hotel qualify on all perspectives. Today the voluminous 1881 **Athenaeum** - the world's first hotel to have electric lights - is a long way from a notorious haunt, and the guests maintaining family tradition by returning summer after summer don't tell each other to "look out for ghosts." In the region around the lake, though, the Athenaeum holds a tradition of hauntings. There is the occasional recent report. A "cold spot" (one of those potentially psychic earmarks) has been noted frequently within the Athenaeum, as is, on occasion, a vigorous poltergeist. (What would you call it when the young staffer's bed shook under him all night, costing him any bit of sleep?) A certain elevator gets a bit of late-night weirdness, and one of the longtime tales concerns a little girl who rode her tricycle into the open doors of it and lost her life down the yawning shaft. Her tender bell can still be heard, on occasion, in many parts of the hotel, as if she is still looking for her family. Even a former manager seems to return to the site of his employment. And the living are beginning to flock here out of season. A revival of sorts is on, making the Institution and its Athenaeum a conference center at other times of the year.

7) Before the building of the Interstate 90, Route 20 was *the* Western Door thoroughfare, and towns like **Fredonia** were living happy days. In the 1930s The White Inn was "discovered" by Duncan Hines and listed in his fifty-strong "Family of Fine Restaurants." Gifted psychics, too, have discovered **The White Inn** on their way to nearby Lily Dale, and on several occasions owner Robert Contuguglia has been told that his building has "presences," fortunately benign ones. (An owner's late-1960s murder-suicide feeds speculation that at

A Tour of Haunts

˜ ˜ ˜ 13 ˜ ˜ ˜

least one influence might be troubled.) Another sour spirit may be that of Isabel White, who sold the home in 1919 and then rocked and scowled at it from the porch next door thereafter, displeased with its conversion to a Classically-inspired inn. (Many presume she's the haunter - one of them, anyway - most fond of "her" room which seems to be #314.) It's called **The White Inn** after Squire White, Mayflower descendant and first doctor in Chautauqua County, who built the home in 1811. In 1868 son Devillo replaced the original wood frame with a solider Victorian Second Empire house, the core of what's standing now. The Inn has 1868 and 1919 wings, and the older hosts most of the psychic events, which include misbehaving appliances, moving furniture (especially in the Presidential Suite!), and several apparitions. One is a young girl, thirteen or so years old, in gauzy white apparel and with long auburn hair. In one report she just stood, arms out and palms uplifted.

8) A lakefront reef-and-beef eatery with a banquet hall and a lively bar, today's **Dock at the Bay** in **Blasdell** is built over and around one of the county's older buildings, the 1805 Willink Hotel. The bay was a major thoroughfare in wartime, and the inn housed many a soldier, at least some of whom seem likely to be coming back. One of the reputed spooks is Captain James Byrd, who fought alongside Admiral Perry on the Niagara River in the War of 1812. Perry's ship anchored in the bay in 1814; Byrd's girlfriend waited at the Willink Hotel; Byrd slipped over the side for a swim and a connubial visit. He was shipboard in a few hours, but he had been missed. He was court-martialed for desertion, shot, and buried in nearby Hamburg. Another Byrd - cousin Amos - fought in the naval battle of Black Rock (same war). His grave is in nearby Bayview, but a piece of his tombstone is part of today's Dock at the Bay. A mid-1800s bar-scuffle spilled outside, destroyed the front steps, and got a piece of Amos Byrd's tombstone shot off. The stone was allegedly refashioned into a Dock at the Bay doorstep. No wonder Byrd spirits are restless, and there may be too many others to count. McKenzie's War was ongoing in 1837 and 1838. On New Year's Day 1838, a band of Americans gathered at Comstock's Tavern (now the Dock at the Bay) for their half-hearted invasion of Canada, and this would have been the last festivity any of the soon-dead remembered. Today the former Willink Hotel is quite proud of its festive spirits. A

hostess calls them "my friends." A bartender hears them calling his name, and few members of the staff lack a story.

9) Down the parkway from Fort Erie is the nearby town of **Black Creek**, which was settled by Loyalists in the late 1700s. Where the Black Creek feeds the Niagara River under the Niagara Parkway is **The Lighthouse**, a tavern-restaurant that opened in 1997 and was named for its cupola with three large lights. Built in the early 1800s, the two-story building has been a lumber mill, a jail, a station on the Underground Railroad, a pub, an ice cream bar, and an inn (at which American President Grover Cleveland met his mistress in the late 19th century). Fort Erie was the bloodiest battle in Canadian history, and if you think of that as a factor in ghost reports, you have your rationale for the spillover to the Lighthouse. Stubborn poltergeist effects were here from the beginning, reported owner Kevin Smith - like lighting and heating systems with ideas of their own. The first customers told Kevin about traditional presences at the inn: "Stella," the nurturing keeper of the the place; and "George," a British soldier in 1812-era garb who comes running with his musket when accidents occur, as they do too frequently on the tricky, scenic parkway. Others hear spirit-children laugh in the breeze. The most curious presences are the passing ones, ones that are only visible as they come in with natural guests, then vanish when inside. Customers report them entering after parkway accidents that set new souls on the loose. Once a tall Black man entered and disappeared. An American looking like him had just lost his life in a wreck nearby. Psychic Gwendolyn Pratt is sure these wanderers are drawn to the lights above, a beacon visible for many miles in this low country along the river. "They come to the first light they see, and from here they find their way home."

10) **Grand Island's Holiday Inn** goes to prove that a building needn't be old to be haunted. One of Western New York's most famous haunted buildings was built around 1973, and ghost stories started almost immediately. (A house-cleaner sensed something odd in a room she was cleaning; the door closed itself, closing her inside; she screamed.) It's entered the folklore that there was a fire on the site back in the 1800s, one that killed a little girl who resembles "Tanya," the specter people see here when they see anything. They even associate her with a girl buried in the nearby Whitchaven Cemetery, a

A Tour of Haunts

~ ~ ~ 15 ~ ~ ~

member of the Nice family. But the historians of Grand Island can't make any such connection to a person or a fire, and there seems to be no good reason at all for the Inn to have a spook, as it seems they do. Room 422 is her favorite spot, but she's all over the Inn. Someone plays after hours in the pool. Someone fools with the elevators and lights. Someone shows a kidlike fascination for contemporary toys. (Once a family woke in the middle of the night to their toddler crying that someone was playing with his toys. The bleary-eyed father saw a small, strange girl at the foot of the bed, one who dematerialized.) Someone even shows up in the stray photograph, the spitting image of the "Tanya" people report. One of the best apparent spirit-photographs I've ever seen in Western New York comes from a 50th wedding anniversary at the Inn. The filmy image of a girl no one saw at the time turned up behind the golden couple in the photo. It's too faint to show up here. It sure looks like a little girl.

11) **Niagara-on-the-Lake** may hold the oldest still-operating Inn in British Canada. Hand-hewn beams and heavy plank floors set down in 1815 "still echo to the sounds of the British soldiers and townsfolk who two centuries ago gathered here for food and drink," says **The Angel Inn** brochure. The Harmonious Coach House (1789) may have preceded it on the site in the original "Butlersburg," named for Lt. Col. John Butler, a roughriding Loyalist guerrilla fighter during the Revolution involved in the infamous Torture Tree incident. In 1813 the retreating Yanks torched all of Newark (Niagara-on-the-Lake's second name). The Harmonious went with it, to the sacrifice of Butler's famed and prized pewter beer mug. The inn was rebuilt on the site by John Ross and named "Angel" in reference to his wife. The old softie. Since the 1820s there's been a ghost here, thought to be that of Captain Colin Swayze. When last in the flesh the resident specter was said to have delayed fleeing the battle to rendezvous with a sweetheart, and was killed in the Inn cellars during the fighting, possibly even "tortured to death by Yanks." (Torture isn't in the Yankee handbook, but if the folks who survived Cherry Valley could have just gotten hold of that Colonel Butler...) Distinct and sometimes heavy footsteps can be heard at the Inn at night, usually in the basement named for Swayze. Sometimes the noble captain appears in the apparent flesh. It's believed that, as long as the British flag flies over the Inn (as it does now) the valorous ghost of Colin

Swayze will do no harm. Tell that to the employees who won't go in the building alone. They get spooked by the phones, ringing sporadically, with no one responding at the other end... by the doors shaking of their own accord.

12) A fast-food restaurant may seem an odd place for a haunting, but this one - a McDonald's - operates in one of the Western Door's oldest buildings. **Lewiston's** 1824 **Frontier House** was once the finest inn west of Albany and the last stop on the Barton Stage Line. It hosted some famous people: James Fenimore Cooper, President McKinley, DeWitt Clinton, James Fenimore Cooper, Henry Clay, Washington Irving, and maybe even the mysterious William Morgan, the Jimmy Hoffa of the mid-nineteenth-century, the Batavia anti-Mason whose 1826 disappearance shocked the nation. Its paranormal pattern preceded its McDonald's term. Apparitions, opening and closing doors in an empty building... The manager himself was once shocked out of his shower by someone outside the steamy panels; he knew he was alone in the building. A maintenance man quit over related creepiness, and the husky of the Frontier House chef got into the act, reacting with alarm to what was, to humans, vacant space. You might think the site's 1977 refashioning into the McDonald's franchise would lessen its psychic vigor, but in the late-70's both employees and workmen at the building sensed it was still psychically active: there were missing tools, misplaced items, and mysteriously opening windows. Some employees of the Lewiston McDonald's still consider it haunted, due to unexplained phenomena of the familiar sort. It may be Morgan's ghost stalking his murderers through this former Masonic meeting hall; a cleaning woman often talked with a man in old-timey clothing she encountered in the nooks, crannies, and closets of the place, and when the Frontier House was remodeled in 1963, many were disappointed that the body of Morgan was not found. The real Morgan is most likely to have been taken to Fort Niagara and done for there, but fort lore doesn't list him among the residents. Considering the spooky folkloric company, I can see why he'd haunt someplace else. The fort's headless ghost wouldn't be much on conversation; that fop of a French count would be tiresome, sashaying around the graveyard and complaining about American foreign policy and how tough it is finding good help; and that hobgoblin jabbering at you all night long...

2
The Haunted Mansion

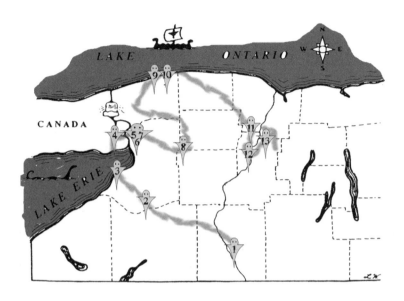

It's probably right to follow with the classic "haunted mansion." Something about big, once-or-currently splendid houses gives people impressions of ghosts the way trees get dogs thinking of relief. Maybe it's shameful for a collector to say, but my choice of haunted mansions has been arbitrary. Western New York has so many to pick from, and I could have gotten ghost stories about almost any of them. I picked a few not-so-famous ones. A few others are so famous it would seem ignorant to leave them out. Let's start our tour at one of the few Western New York sites to make it into Louis C. Jones' *Things That Go Bump in the Night*.

1) **Wellsville** holds one of Western New York's most famous haunts, a proverbially spooky Victorian at the corner of West State Street and Brooklyn Avenue. Known for its arresting wedding-cake allure, **The Pink House** - named for its major color and frosted white with balconies and windows - was built in 1869 by Edwin Bradford Hall. The folklore gives it a host of spooks, with a love triangle behind them. (An older sister jilted for a younger. A suicide, a ghost that led a child to her death...) Not really, but there is a dateable tragedy from which it all sprouted, the 1907 drowning of a two-year-old in

the Pink House's fountain as her wheelchair-bound grandfather watched. The house is still the subject of neighborhood folklore, potential poltergeist trickery, and images on the lawn by the site of the missing fountain. For all its regional prominence and national reputation, the Pink House is a curious site. You have to probe to get witnesses to talk, and not all of them are convinced that it's haunted.

2) Built about 1880 and called **The Gardiniere House** (after a family who owned it in the 1900s), the former home of John P. Myers was the first private residence in **Springville** with a telephone, and one of the first with indoor plumbing. Civil War veteran Myers was one of the heavy hitters in town, and his home at the corner of East Main and Elk was a focus of town society. It was Myers who, with a fellow veteran, commissioned the monument to Springville residents lost in the Civil War. (Somehow only the two benefactors were mentioned, and a recent campaign raised enough to have the names of those actually killed in the war etched on the stone in the small town park.) While heading to New York in 1895 on his fifty-second July 4 birthday, Myers disappeared with $25,000 in his pocket. Springville people aren't sure what he was doing with all that cash, or where he may have ended up. Some suspect a getaway to exotic climes, but most conjecture something sadder and more prosaic: that this man who as a youth survived the Andersonville POW camp was knocked off in his middle-age with all that green in his bag and rests now under some rock in the woods. The mansion he left behind is not hard to sell or rent, but... People see things here. Dogs react to invisible presences; the occasional guest just can't stay here; and people in the street occasionally spot a girl in the tower. Maybe she's one of Myers' daughters, still waiting for him to come back with that 25K.

3) Young East Coast salesman Darwin Martin learned business under Elbert Hubbard's wing. When Hubbard left the Larkin Soap Company to found East Aurora's Roycroft, Martin filled his mentor's shoes. By 1926 Martin was one of the richest men in Buffalo, and hired illustrious architect Frank Lloyd Wright to design their lakeshore summer home in **Derby**. Mr. Martin the businessman was concerned about costs; Mrs. Martin the Christian Scientist was concerned about "sacred space," an aura that's step one with all Wright buildings. She admired the megalithic mood of the mounded

A Tour of Haunts

circle at the Lake Placid (NY) Club. At **Graycliff** the impression was achieved with a circular pond, routing the approach to the mansion in the direction Wright (ever-conscious of pathways and progresses) favored. This integration of house and site is something Wright would never surpass. Maybe it was a little too integrated; this is largely a summer community, and Graycliff was designed for summer living. The Lake Erie gales drove second owners the Piarist Fathers to winterize, and some of the changes they made so outraged Wright that he stormed through it in 1958 with 25 apprentices, yelled "This is not mine!" handed the priests his card, and demanded to be hired to set things right, including building them a proper chapel. To him the priests had ruined the most important part of the house, its ability to be part of the horizon. The Fathers kept their own council on the matter and Wright passed into spirit six months later. Today the Graycliff Conservancy lovingly runs the house and keeps an uneasy lid on the ghost stories. Nevertheless, they are here. Even Conservancy members who have spent nights at Graycliff experience an amazing feeling of vitality about the house, as if the structure itself comes to life, creaking and chirping like a night-time forest. Others who stay here report imposing apparitions they sense might be the Martins.

4) Head to the Erie, then stay on the water till you come up the Niagara River. Bertie Hall (1826) on the Niagara Parkway was deeply involved in the seminal events of Canada and the Niagara Peninsula. Its Scottish-American builder William Forsyth was a venturesome rogue often on the outs with the law. Its many owners included the Fenian Raiders, who commandeered the landmark for their headquarters during the 1866 siege of **Fort Erie**. Today's **Mildred M. Mahoney Dolls' House Gallery** is a "rare example of the Greek Revival Style" and a great collector of spook lore, much of which harks to the role of an alleged tunnel beneath it in smuggling and human traffic. Its landing was said to be just below the Bertie house. Forsyth children were rumored drowned in it, and two family deaths in the river are known. Dollhouse lore features few apparitions, but the notion of a haunting is long-settled. Once a medium gave us impressions that have settled into folklore. "David" is a little boy allegedly drowned in the tunnel. "All he wants is attention," said a member of the staff who named him. Psychic reports include rapping sounds, electrical pranks, a malfunctioning video camera,

and sweet lilac-smells, usually after the stairtop apparition of a flower-bearing woman. The occasional display gets torn up overnight. People who live near the Dollhouse describe noises, even laughter, coming from it at night, when everyone knows it has no human dwellers. Some narrow the focus to a single dollhouse within it, the Pink Colonial. Made in 1924, its living room furnishings include a tiny Ouija board. It's often found in the morning in a new location, moved overnight... in an empty building.

5) Built over the pre-1820 Black Rock cemetery, **Allentown's** Symphony Circle may be steeped in spirits. One majestic house overlooking it - the Queen Anne brick at 26 Richmond - has a long haunted reputation. Allentown old-timers call it **The Maytham Mansion** after the Great Lakes shipping family that built it in 1892. (Its architect may have been Edward Kent.) It's been home to several prominent families, as well as freelance desperadoes during bouts of vacancy. It was also *El Nathan* ("Gift of God"), a home for poor women, some of whom may have been impaired. [Miracles like those of Father Baker (empty larders magically replenished, cash donated in times of crisis) were reported of founder Abigail Luffe.] The home is built in twin parts, and has other intrigue. Entrances to basement tunnels are boarded over, and the inner layout winds. Its term as the Buffalo Philharmonic Orchestra's administration offices may have been its psychic flowering. An impish prankster routinely disarranged the desks of neat-freaks. Cold spots were reported, with such frequent electrical pranks that new hires got schooled on the circuit-breakers. Apparitions include a little girl at the top of the stairs (reputedly caught once on film), and a stern, silent older woman who comes to the door on misty days. An internal memo even addressed the matter, and, as part of a Halloween 1992 stint, a psychic couple studied it along with WGR radio personality Tom Bauerle. (Odd effects did surface under the the 1992 examination, particularly when the tapes were replayed.)

6) One publication claims that **Allentown's** Second Empire-style **Coatsworth Mansion** was built in 1869. Another judges it ten years younger. What's not in doubt is the impression the Cottage Street house makes on the kids of the neighborhood; they call it "the Castle," a fitting nickname for a place under whose entry a coat of arms is carved, those of the

A Tour of Haunts

Nevilles, under which the Coatsworth family claimed to have fought on the winning side of the Wars of the Roses. Like many buildings with haunted reputations, the Coatsworth had former occupants who were "watchers," people who spent time in one significant part of the building, on the lookout for something. Owner Coatsworth was said to have built the octagonal tower so he could see his ships come in the harbor. Also typical of haunted buildings, this splendid one has gone through periods of neglect, during which leagues of stoners and what-have-you made it their home-in-place-of-home. At one point the Coatsworth was owned by the Church and tenanted by the Brothers of Mercy and Carmelite Nuns, who may figure among the haunters. It was later bought for only a few thousand dollars, revamped, and used as apartments. The lore of the Coatsworth includes cold spots, unexplained noises, and apparitions visible from within and without. The image of an austere old dame, possibly one of the nuns who had once lived here, is strong in the folklore. We interviewed one former tenant who saw her reflection behind him as he was shaving. She looked "dead," he said, trying to be funny, but his meaning was clear; and he's not the only one who's seen her.

7) "The House of Light," it was called, **The Mansion** at 414 Delaware, one of **Buffalo's** finest Second-Empire-style mansard homes (1870). (Its architect was George Allison.) Since *Banner of Light* was the longtime Spiritualist paper, this name suggests a Spiritualist influence, and the house known by it may have had three owners in its first year. Builder and grain elevator tycoon Charles Sternberg may never have lived in it, and John Condit Smith died quickly after taking it over. Third owner Samuel Curtis Trubee turned it into a fine family hotel that hosted luminaries during the Pan-Am Exposition. Like many Buffalo buildings, this one has gone a course of disuse and multiple functions, and by the 1930's it was even rumored a bordello. Legendary Buffalo bon vivant Hugo DiGiulio came along and brought us the inimitable Victor Hugo's supperclub (1947-1977). Regular performers/overnight guests included Liberace and Howard Keel. Another period of darkness followed during which its haunted reputation may have started. By the late 1990s Gino Principe commenced the long restoration process, during which people stopped him in supermarkets with tales from the fallow periods. Apparitions, spontaneous fires, and even

strange images of light just above the someday-to-be Mansion figure in neighborhood tradition. Many photos taken inside the building during the restoration have "orbs" - balls of light - which some ghosthunters consider budding ghost-forms. Today's exquisite "The Mansion at Delaware" seems visited by an array of harmless effects and a pair of phantoms, at least one of which may be the "little girl" archetype so familiar to ghostlore. (Those in Buffalo alone could put together a Brownie troop.) I hear both Faith Hill and Eric Clapton stayed here during Buffalo visits. Though there's no reason to think they were together, I'm jealous enough of the possibility to take it up with Ol' Slowhand at the next ultra-hip party to which local ghosthunters are always being invited.)

8) Head east of the city till you come to **Cowlesville** and one of Wyoming County's most illustrious homes. Frances Folsom - the 21-year-old granddaughter of builder John B. Folsom - raised eyebrows at her 1886 marriage to her father's law partner, the 49-year-old bachelor President Grover Cleveland, who had visited the 1835 **Folsom House** often. She must have been a looker, Oscar Folsom's daughter; she was lively and bright, said all of Washington. Only the death of her grandfather prevented the marriage from taking place in the Folsom House. This Federal Greek Revival home has also been an inn and maybe a general store; but its most startling guests may be of another time and place. Ghosts have been reported in the house, among them a mystery woman visible only to animals and young children; but the most dramatic psychic effects may come from outside it. In fact, the whole ridge may be haunted. One stern, dark-coated, top-hatted man appears on the hill above Folsomdale Road at night, maybe even stalking unwary kids. (Some wonder if this is Ephraim Barry, buried fully dressed in his bed half a mile away.) "The Egg Lady" is an early morning specter in skirt and shawl always walking away from the observer. The locals had gotten used to her, but she and other spooks seem to have steadily lost energy since the 1950s. Most of our witnesses haven't seen these apparitions since their childhood.

9) **Newfane's** 1820 **Van Horn Mansion** is another of the Western Door's more famous haunts. "Green Acres" was the name of the red brick home on the Transit Road when James Van Horn and his family lived in it. It's had several uses

A Tour of Haunts

since, including a mid-twentieth century stint as a restaurant. The Newfane Historical Society cares for it lovingly today. About a hundred feet off is "Cemetery Orchard" and the marker of Malinda, wife of James Van Horn, Jr. The stone may mark either the spot of her rest or the blow (from a falling branch) that sent her to it, at twenty-one, in 1837. It's she many suspect is behind the haunting. The apparitions include a man and a woman, both looking out of place in our century, and a mysterious child. The children of a family who lived here in the 1950s could not sleep in a certain room, claiming to be troubled by *the others*. Some of the liveliest stories came from the empty periods. Roofers noted spectral faces looking out of the windows. Motorists skidded to avoid hitting a little girl who ran from the mansion and then vanished. Carpenters fled when someone materialized out of a cloud in a bedroom. Moving lights were reported inside the dark mansion. Even today bands of amateur psychics meet regularly in the Van Horn mansion, and some of them have recorded amazing effects, including rapping sounds that seemed to communicate, claiming to be a little old lady named "Abigail," quite happy at Green Acres. She can't be the only spirit here. Malinda must be in the mix.

10) On clear days we can see, they say, Toronto across the lake from its cupola; and on all of them its former tenants - the Sisters of St. Joseph - peer through all impediments into realms above; but the past of the place Niagara County natives call "The Hoodoo House" is dark, and most of its details are cloudy. Somehow the notion of a deadly curse got into local tradition, and most of its paraphernalia - haunted stones, sudden deaths, self-opening doors, regular specters, and disastrous fires - made their way into *World Magazine's* bold and elaborate story (May 17, 1908) about **Appleton Hall** in **Olcott**. At first the home of early settler Shubal Merritt, the house may have burned and been rebuilt in 1853 by a well-heeled Merritt daughter. Multiple owners, strange deaths, and periods of vacancy figure in decades of legends. Strange lights were reported of the cupola at night, and one lonely and mordant tenant even scratched his deathbed lament on a window in the hall. The unexplained death of a beloved doctor here was the last straw for the county residents, and the folkloric case for the Hoodoo House was sealed. Paranormal reports lasted into the first quarter of the twentieth century until the pious Sisters took over. They may just be the smoke

concealing fire; but still, let's leave this as an example of a country version of an urban legend. I'm not sure at all what's behind the stories.

11) Devout Spiritualist Erastus Hyde built **The Octagon House** about 1870 in the small Allegany County town of Friendship. He and his wife held many seances in it and died only two days apart in 1931. The house fell into vacancy and disrepair, and the stories started: strange sounds, moving objects, and spectral pow-wows. Then it was moved to **Mumford's** Genesee Country Village, more or less a museum community dedicated to pioneer life. Paranormal stories started again as soon as it arrived: moving tools and objects, agitated dogs, unsettling dreams, and creeped-out visitors. Its octagonal design may have some effect on the folklore. The eight-sided shape often used in sacred architecture tends to gather supernatural rumor, and the Western Door has a number of octagonal buildings, a form advocated by Burned-over District mystic Orson Fowler (1809-1887), founder of several enlightened settlements. An octagon house was built in Lily Dale for the Spiritualist headquarters. Akron's Rich House is another, and I've heard of a contemporary community near Attica based around an octagonal structure.

12) One of a long line of Yalies - grandfather and uncle were in the first New Haven graduating class - gentleman farmer William Augustus Mills (1777-1844) was the first Euroamerican to settle in this part of the Genesee Valley in 1790. He built his stately **Mt. Morris** home in 1838 and enjoyed his role as retired War of 1812 general, reviewing parades on the village green before his house, looking every inch the old hero in his medals, his plumes, his epaulets, his scarf, everything flowing triumph and color, his sword seeming to catch the sun's glow and cast it to the rows of passing bayonets. Wounded in hot action on the Niagara Frontier, General Mills was no paper tiger. And he and his parading comrades were far from the first to enjoy living with an overlook of the Genesee Valley. The 14-room house nicknamed the **Mills Mansion** was in the Mills family till 1923. It was divided into apartments, and in 1946 a factory nearby started using the building as a warehouse. It fell vacant by the mid-1950s, and its only occupants for 20 years were pigeons. The spooklore probably comes from the vacant period. Something fixed the impression firmly in the minds of the

A Tour of Haunts

community. Volunteer archaeologists Andy Schelz and Justin Tubiolo stayed here on occasion while doing the dig, and people told them to beware of the ghosts. This site is interesting as a folklore-producer because of what's underneath it. While excavating for the various outbuildings associated with the mansion, archaeologists discovered that this was a dwelling and flint-working place as far back as four thousand years. (Flint tools and projectile points of the Brewerton culture were found here.) The Mills Mansion was actually built on the site of a huge burial mound - 8 to 10 feet high and nearly a hundred in diameter - of some unknown culture. About 1820 the mound was removed, and many artifacts came out, including, says Livingston County historian Lockwood Doty (1876), a human skeleton so big its jaw fit like a mask over the face of the county's biggest man.

13) Some of the most persistent folkloric accounts of ghosts in the Genesee Valley come from the **Spencer/Chandler Mansion** near the Abbey by Rt. 63, between **Geneseo** and Pifford. Julia Tyler - a sister of President John Tyler - became the wife of William Spencer of Geneseo. This southern belle was very unhappy in the north and died sometime around the Civil War. When that tragic and gruesome conflict was over, her brothers transferred her remains to a Richmond, VA, cemetery. She was resting with no "damn Yankees." (Though first use of that phrase is attributed to Red Jacket, it was recruited for use by many Southerners.) Julia may not rest so peacefully there, either. She's been reported on the Main Street of Geneseo, as well as roundabout her former mansion. Local rumor has it that the Spencer/Chandler Mansion was so deviled by visions and effects that an exorcist was summoned in the 1980s. They say this one refused to enter the mansion because he sensed some "threatening presence." (Why else would you send for an exorcist? It's like an exterminator refusing to answer a call because he's afraid of bugs.) We heard this from the historians, and maybe it's all true, but it sounds like one of those tall tales that gravitates to suspected paranormal sites.

3
College Spirit

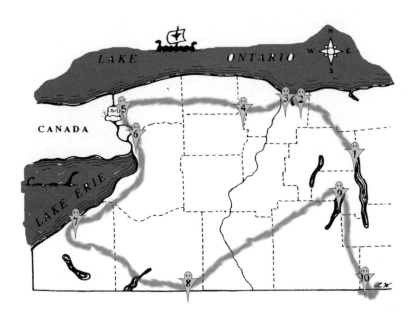

We almost didn't do this chapter. It was shooting fish in a barrel. Every college has a haunted building, and the students love prodigies so much that they circulate all the stories. Since few readers are exposed to this tradition, the subject needed addressing. Here's a sample of the Western Door's college hauntings.

1) Let's start in **Geneva** on the shores of Seneca Lake. Even he website of **Hobart & William Smith Colleges** admits that three halls - Blackwell, McCormick, and Miller Houses - may be visited by ghosts. Footsteps when the houses are empty, shadowy heads floating through walls, and windows opening and shutting with no visible causes would say "spooks" to me. A prominent website reports poltergeist activity about even a fourth, Hirschson Hall, even giving us the room (#304). This has to be a record. If asked to speculate about the psychic energy at this college, I think I'd point out that it rests upon the legendary shores of Seneca Lake, an apparent "X-Zone" of its own.

A Tour of Haunts

2) Move on up the 90 to **Rochester** and young **St. John Fisher College**, whose upperclassmen are traditionally housed in Dorsey Hall. In the shape of an extended V, Dorsey's rooms are the only ones on campus with their own bathrooms, which makes this a very private and quiet dorm... One would think. But Dorsey has the campus reputation of having "company." Many students have claimed to see apparitions here in random rooms and halls, but the lounge area on the first floor of Dorsey and the lobby near it is the focus of some of the best reports. Now and then something that happens here is so unlikely that it seems paranormal. One incident sounding like a poltergeist prank involved ID cards and scanners, resulting in the misidentification of a certain female student in connection with a case of vandalism. (Witnesses confirmed that she was in her room during the event.) Sometimes late at night, people in this lobby who think their talk is private get a sick feeling of being lewdly watched. They turn to look, all around. It's then that some of them notice red "eyes" that seem to form in the glass walls of the lounge.

3) Western New York is widely associated with the Seneca and other Iroquois nations. The traditional home of their Algonquin foes was Canada and the Northeast. There were, however, many Native American nations here; and there was Algonquin settlement on Pinnacle Hill in **Rochester**. Its heyday was probably the European Middle Ages, around the 1200s. Today the **University of Rochester** occupies the hill of their former home, and a number of its buildings are thought haunted. The specter of the Rush Rhees Library may have its origin in more recent events. The old stacks are said to be visited by the apparition of a workman who died during its construction in 1929. Even the campus newspaper has reported numerous sightings over the years. Those stacks used to be open...

4) **SUNY at Brockport** is on the original campus of a pair of earlier schools, a Baptist academy and then the Brockport Collegiate Institute (1841). Said to harbor a couple of ghosts, today's Hartwell Hall was built on top of them. Cleaning staff over the years have claimed to experience spooky things in the building, including periodic flurries of activity on one of the upper halls - doors opening and closing, faint laughter, voices - as if spirits were changing classes. Another staffer

swore she was touched on the shoulder while cleaning a classroom, only to turn and find no one. Once she slipped from her stepladder in one of the ballet rooms and was caught and set down gently by an invisible force. Workers are sure they've heard the splashing of ghostly water in an empty pool in the basement. As if that weren't enough, the levitating psychic Phil Jordan studied at Brockport in the 1970s and became a legend for his abilities.

5) It's little wonder that **Niagara University** - at the highest point of the sublime Niagara Gorge in **Niagara Falls** - could attract ghostlore, and we even have a name for the ghost of its most impressive hall. In the fire of December 5, 1864, the unfortunate Thomas Hopkins, a seminary student from Brooklyn, was too zealous in his efforts to save the books of the medieval-style Clet ("clay") Hall, and he was buried in a collapsing wall. I can't say they ever see an apparition that looks like Hopkins, but students here attribute every creak and crackle to the resident spirit. Today poltergeist phenomena of the usual type - footsteps, electrical pranks, self-operating faucets, self-opening doors, even faint laughter - are hallmarks of the friendly presence. Even metallic clanking sounds - like the venerable rattling chains - come from below the theater in Clet Hall.

6) Human Dimensions Institute (HDI) started in 1967 as a lecture series at Rosary Hill (now **Daemen**) College in **Amherst**, then run by Franciscan nuns. HDI studied various spiritual philosophies and did lab research in areas of health, hypnosis, ESP, and the dream-experience. By the late-1970s HDI had spun off and relocated to North Carolina under its new name VERITAS, but it left one heck of a haunted hall behind, about which a campus tradition has sprouted. Before it was college property Curtiss Hall was a fine home owned by two brothers who didn't get along. They lived in separate sides of the house, and one (failing in his attempt to kill the other) finally killed himself. People on campus say the pair of them haunts the hall, and security staff are familiar with the reports. Footsteps pound in the attic; empty halls flourish images; books fly off of basement shelves and seemingly aim themselves at people, which is very rare in this kind of research. One new professor was actually warned about the ghosts at Curtiss Hall by members of campus security. She didn't believe they were joking.

A Tour of Haunts

· · · 29 · · ·

7) In September of 1970 **SUNY Fredonia's** big dorm was so new its wings (including Igoe Hall) were known by letters. The college got round to naming them and polled the student body for ideas. Tribute seemed in order for Buffalonian Jimmy Igoe, a popular sophomore-to-be who had lost his life the July before in a boating accident on Lake Erie. The psychic effects started that autumn with the former Hall E (which Jimmy would have occupied) and continue today as a leisurely infestation of poltergeists. "Hi, Jimmy!" the students call out merrily to anything unexplained, though some others are still shocked. No one reports the actual ghost of Jimmy Igoe here, either; but where images are concerned, his picture has to be treated with respect. Once residents of another wing stole the portrait of Jimmy Igoe, and paranormal "chaos erupted," in the words of an article in the campus paper. It was returned the next day, and so far as I know it's been sacrosanct since. Even the most irreverent human pranksters don't mess with it.

8) Dating to the mid-1800s, Devereaux Hall is one of the oldest buildings at **St. Bonaventure University** in **Olean**. (Campus sources claim not to be sure of the date, and the students joke that they don't want anybody to know so as to inspire no extra complaints from people being housed there.) The attic-like space of the fifth floor was the site of a seance and possibly a black mass held by some students in the mid-1960s. The amateur magicians spooked themselves, ran out, and were expelled, but legions of students afterward report strange noises coming from the unoccupied fifth floor. People outside it witness unexplained lights, sometimes on the top floor. Father Alphonsus Trabold - a believer in psychic phenomena - considered the flap surrounding "Fifth Dev" all make-believe. He should know. "Father Al" taught religion and parapsychology at Bonny for a long time. He would have been the exorcist had an exorcism been needed in the last half-century on the Niagara Frontier. Still, that hasn't stopped the development of "Fifth Dev" folklore. It's hard to find a student here who hasn't heard some story about the hauntings, and hard to miss one who hasn't had some experience with Fifth Dev.

9) The oldest building on the campus of **Keuka College** in **Keuka Park** is named for its founding president George Ball.

His 1907 death seems to have released the fun side of him, or so the folklore has it. Word is that Ball Hall has been the focus of expression for some adolescent semi-physical prankster. As of the late 1990s, even the public relations department acknowledged the psychic reports on campus, in which surprise elevator joy-rides figure prominently. One of the reports might qualify as paranormal. The elevator is programmed to go up only three floors, but once in a while someone ends up in the empty attic, rumored to be Ball's haunt. "The elevator took me to the attic and the door opened in total darkness," a former student told the *Rochester Democrat & Chronicle* in 1993. "I ran in the corner so I wouldn't have to look into the darkness." Those who live on the third floor of Ball Hall often complain of loud footsteps on their ceiling, the floor of the empty attic.

10) Just south of the Finger Lakes wine-making region, **Elmira College** started in 1855 as the first accredited all-women college in the United States. (It went co-ed in 1969.) Eight of its buildings are listed on the National Register of Historic Places, and it may have a couple of haunted halls, according to a prominent website listing New York State haunts. Today Elmira is 42 scenic acres, but once the original college was held within a single hall named for Elmira's first president Dr. Augustus Cowles. At Cowles Hall lights - "orbs" - are reported floating down halls of the building, and whispering is heard when there are no people around. The building feels unusual to some folks and is reputed to be split down the middle into "evil" and "good" sides. (That's being dramatic. I think it's all neutral.) An empty room on the fourth floor may be the focus of the haunting of Tompkins Hall. Lights turn themselves on in this room even when it's locked and empty. Campus folklore attributes the haunting in some fashion to a female student who died on campus and associates her with a portrait that once hung near the troubled room. But why take my word for it? There's a website devoted to the spooks of Elmira College; let's all defer to their judgement.

4
Grave Haunts

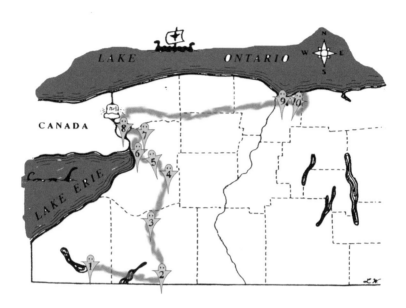

It seems almost too obvious to look for ghosts in graveyards. It's also counterintuitive. Except for British and Continental Romantic-era poets... Shelley, Novalis... Would anyone with a choice hang out there? My disembodied spirit would go farther afield looking for entertainment. Libraries. Theaters. The All-England Tennis Club during the Wimbledon fortnight. I could finish *A Glastonbury Romance*. I could at least stand a chance at getting into the Oscar parties... Nevertheless, the haunted graveyard is a fixture of literature, and some burying-grounds do get reputations of being haunted. This book would be incomplete without surveying those of Western New York. Let's start in the Southern Tier.

1) **Frewsburg's Gurnsey Hollow Cemetery** gives many people creepy feelings. More than one of them have contacted me hoping I can explain them. I regret to say that it's hard to take many of the reports seriously. Like the Goodleberg Cemetery in Wales, Gurnsey Hollow has become a high school party-place. Coming here to dare a supposed psychic experience is almost a rite of passage for some teens, who propagate much of the lore. (Kiss the marker at the gate before you leave Gurnsey Hollow, or... *you DIE!!!!*) The inter-

net gossip about this site is pretty wild. The tradition of a single haunter has built up, often a differently-abled boy whom the other children tormented and finally stoned to death. In other versions of the tale, the stoning victim/cemetery haunter is a young lady of "the 1800s" who is buried here. There's murk, however, at the root of the matter. Historians aren't sure anybody got stoned here in the literal sense. The cemetery itself dates from the 1830s; it's remote, and hasn't been used for burials in decades. There's no doubt about the force of the folklore, though, which includes glowing graves, flying balls of light, crucified animals, and mystery-children laughing and playing in the rural surroundings. There may have been old Native American earthworks nearby, and, though this is a cliche, that may be the source of the folklore if not the psychic "energy" behind it.

2) Between the Civil War and the Great Depression Irish immigrants lived in a community in today's Allegany State Park. So little is left of "New Ireland" that it can be a chore to find it, but it exerts an almost mystical call to the descendants of its settlers, many of whom are buried in **St. Patrick's Cemetery** in **Limestone**. Rather than outright spookery, the graveyard here seems associated with subtle, even touching psychic effects, like odd communications to the living as if the old sleepers here had something to say. For instance, a small research team sought a specific New Ireland stone among the weathered hundreds here; one of their dogs led them to it, circling the stone and barking, as if dog and spirit had colluded. Another case involved a brother and sister praying to find their elderly father, lost in the vast park looking for New Ireland, his childhood home. Hundreds of searchers had missed him, but after this moment of guidance, his children found him where he had fallen... home.

3) A few yards off of a hilly road by the Griffis Sculpture Park is a tiny cemetery, just a stone, actually, the grave of The **Ashford Hollow** Witch. The inscription reads: Lewis Disch, 1794-1882; Salome Disch, 1798-1862; Sophia Disch, 1833-1909. There must have been a sense of otherness about Sophie, the family's only, spinster daughter. She made her way selling dairy products to a cheese factory. Maybe she liked it that way, alone. Long-living in the woody hills might have gnarled her personality as much as her appearance. From somewhere it got started that she was a witch. As recently as

A Tour of Haunts

° ° ° 33 ° ° °

the 1970s old-timers remembered the woman with the craggy appearance and the big dog. When they found her dead at her house, possibly of a heart attack while chopping wood - at 76 - she was wearing thirteen petticoats, doubtless to keep warm. Something about Sophie draws talk nearly a century after her death. One old photo of the witch's grave showed an odd path ringing it, coming and returning from the trees. There was the hint of a beaten arc about it when last I saw it in April 2001. What procession comes to it from the woods? Who or what dances here midnights?

4) The early nineteenth-century graveyard on **Fish Hill** in **Wales** is an old one for this part of the country. It's also small and wild, flanked by woods and on a steep hill. It's been the scene of tragedies, including the nineteenth-century murder of a Seneca man, tied to a tree by drunken vigilantes in sight of the stones; and the more recent dumping of a gunshot victim in the ravine by his Rochester assailant (still jailed as of 2003). The impression of something else creepy about Fish Hill is strong in local folklore. Strange walking shadows and unexplained voices are among the complaints of visitors, as well as floating light-spheres. Simply standing in a circle of dead trees in the nearby wood made a witness' hair stick straight up one queer fall afternoon that lacked the normal day-sounds. "You have to experience it," she said of Fish Hill. It's striking to consider that Fish Hill could be overshadowed by another cemetery within walking distance, but it seems to be the case. The burying-ground near the **Goodleberg** family home had become a legendary haunt (as well as a high school party place) by the 1960s. The impression of the area as a scene of awe may start with its name, meaning, in German, "Hill of the Ghouls." Mysterious lights, distant crying babies, and classic "Black dog" apparitions are among the reports. Stay away from both of these places. One May Eve in the late 1990s some high school fools dug a cone into Goodleberg, six feet wide and six-deep, attempting to get at the grave of a girl who'd died as a toddler. On the summer solstice 2003 the place claimed another victim, a ghosthunter struck by a car. The investigation into that one is ongoing. Did something drive him into the road?

5) One of the most historic haunted cemeteries in Western New York is **West Seneca's Old Main**, a small plain thing relative to the whopping legends. There's a vacant plot in the

center once marked by a fence, and it may be the grave of a witch. In 1821 a Seneca woman named Kauquatau was executed on the banks of the Cazenovia Creek not far from this village burying-ground. She was likely buried under her cabin, one the Seneca weren't sorry to hand over when the Ebenezers (a German religious community) bought their chunk of the Buffalo Creek Reservation two decades later. The Western New York winter obliged the Ebenezers to use every bit of shelter standing, and one cabin - you guessed it - seemed bedeviled by supernatural effects: terrible sounds and hideous apparitions. The cabin was burned, the ground consecrated, and the site made part of the Ebenezers' own burial ground. But no one was ever buried on that precise spot - no one, perhaps, but its haunter, whom many presume was the spirit of Kauquatau, convicted witch. It's a string of association, mind you, all hinging on each individual point, but historians familiar with the case have made it. This cemetery has a long record of twentieth-century ghost sightings, some of them written up in local papers.

6) A lot of the region's history slept in the **Buffum Street Cemetery** off of Seneca Street in **Buffalo**. Across from the old "Indian" school and at the mouth of an Olmsted park (Cazenovia), it was the resting place of many prominent Native Americans (including Red Jacket) and the "White Woman of the Genesee" Mary Jemison before the supposed relocation of most of its tenants to Forest Lawn. (Jemison was probably conveyed in toto to Letchworth, but some Native American friends doubt that all of Red Jacket got where he was supposed to be headed.) A surprising number of households neighboring this graveyard report small, random effects - moving objects around the house, electrical phenomena, sometimes unexplained sounds. The occasional shadowy trespasser often appears in someone's living room or hallway. The Buffum Street yard features one of the few known ancient earthworks still intact in Western New York, though it's settled quite a bit over time. The mound is so sloping and shallow now that it could be mistaken for a small natural rise. This burying-ground looks so much like a park that it should attract kids from neighborhoods around. People who live near Buffum Street notice that very few of them ever play here. Sometimes dogs that pass this open space with their masters snarl and back away from it as if it held some energy that scared them.

A Tour of Haunts

7) The daddy of them all may be **Forest Lawn**, evidently a power-center for millennia. Big earthworks were noted here by some of the early observers of **Buffalo**, at least one of which was thought to represent a mass burial after a battle between the Iroquois and the Kahquas (the "Neutral" Nation). The area was used as camps and burying-grounds during the War of 1812 and was part of the city landscaped into Fredrick Law Olmsted's design. Park and graveyard could have been crafted with the point of focusing natural-spiritual energy, and Forest Lawn hosts a profusion of sacred architecture. (One famous grave is even aligned like ancient British megaliths so beams of sunlight fall into it on the special day.) Forest Lawn may have several spooks. Cemetery workers talk about an old-timey phantom car that at least once led pursuers through the winding roads of the grounds. During a 1980s chase its 1940s-style taillights seemed to grin at them like a Jack-o-lantern. Besides the sense of shadowy groups of people off in the twilight, at night in Forest Lawn they also report the famous "little girl" ghost. Forest Lawn's is barefoot, white-gowned, and pathetic. When I hear people throwing in these LGG's (little-girl ghosts) I'm always more suspicious; this is surely the most famous ghostly archetype. (The little-girl ghosts in Buffalo alone have a pen-pal club which, through "automatic writing," launched a write-in campaign to elect the Backstreet Boys mayor.) The one at Forest Lawn, however, may be a little more interesting, if only for the quality of the reports. She's been spotted for at least half a century by visitors and staff here alike, and there are living eyewitnesses. There are also outwardly unrelated stories in the region of a little girl "vanishing hitchhiker" spotted near the Delaware Avenue entrance to the cemetery. At least one of them was reported to the police.

8) One of Western New York's most famous haunts - **Grand Island's** Holiday Inn - is in easy walking distance of another ghostlore-battery, the **Whitehaven Cemetery**. The folklore makes a connection. At the Inn they call their little-girl spook "Tanya." A host of apparent misapprehensions about her have been started, among them the impression that she died in a fire on the site and was buried in Whitehaven Cemetery. Popular folklore identifies her with a member of the Nice family whose gravestone allegedly glows on the occasional night. Grand Island historians dispute even the material facts of the argument, knowing of no child-deaths on the spot and

no lethal fires. On the other hand, desperate squatters did live here in the 1800s, and nearby is the spot on the riverbanks where most of the suicides wash up. Other reputed ghosts in Whitehaven Cemetery include a young female AIDS-victim and a man who died in the first Gulf War. (She walks around holding her infant son and he's looking for his pregnant wife. Why haven't they met up by now? This could be a match made in... Heaven.)

9) Burying-grounds often draw supernatural gossip, but the process started at a spot in **Rochester** long before its use as the **Mt. Hope Cemetery**. Near the intersection of Mt. Hope and Elmwood Avenues is a zone considered so haunted by the city's first White settlers that even practical working folk with heavy loads drove carts and wagons far out of their way to avoid it. Since the early 1800s strange lights have been reported at night about the region, floating above the bushes and sometimes drifting skyward. Screams and groans were heard in the nearby swamp. A depression in the cemetery near Dell Avenue nicknamed "the Devil's Punch Bowl" has long been the site of stories about buried treasure. Even meetings of witch-covens have been rumored of Mt. Hope.

10) Talk about a haunted city! Along with legions of rumors of the by-now familiar type, **Rochester's Holy Sepulchre Cemetery** seems to have a phantom hitchhiker of old repute, the foreboding "Lady in Gray," whose wonted stops are on Lake or Dewey Avenues. Holy Sepulchre may also hold the grave of Jack the Ripper, the world's most famous uncaught serial murderer. Rochester resident "Doctor" Francis Tumblety fit all the specs of the unknown London killer. He was even caught and questioned, and Scotland Yard thought they had their man; but he got out on bail and took off. Murders of the Ripper-type broke out at points along his roundabout course back to the states. His name is misspelled ("Tumuelty") on the pink quartz obelisk of the family plot. Ironically, an exact century after the Ripper's London atrocities, murders of the same type broke out in Rochester, maybe spiritually inspired to avenge the sepulchral typos. With avenging specters like "The White Lady of Irondequoit" at the lakeshore and the Lady in Gray patrolling Holy Sepulchre, the Ripper better keep himself planted.

5
Holy Spirits

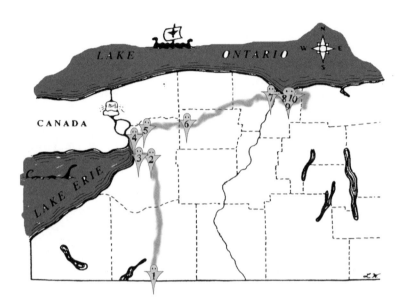

"What church doesn't have a ghost?" said somebody I interviewed while working on this book. As I've said, churches - and buildings built like churches - often get the reputations of being haunted. Western New York has hundreds of churches, and so many of them draw folklore that I can profile just a smattering of the remarkable sites. Let's start just over the border in the Southern Tier.

1) In the first week of 1997 ten thousand people may have visited **Holy Family Western Orthodox Church** in **Bradford**, PA. This small church just over the border from Jamestown was open 24 hours a day after mystery-footsteps summoned the Reverend Robert James to the sanctuary. A smell of roses greeted him, and when he looked around he noticed the images on the camel-colored wallpaper in the corner of the church sanctuary. People saw a variety of shapes: a cross, crossed swords, angels, the Virgin Mother and Child, Joseph, and even Jesus Himself. To some, the images even changed as they were studied. Official Church reaction was subdued. "There probably isn't anything there of religious significance," said one of the four members of the church's Council of Bishops from San Francisco. Sources I trust agree with

them. Reverend James was relocated shortly after and little more made of the matter.

2) The former domain of the religious Ebenezer Society has sprouted hauntings and healings. Them we'll discuss later. But a curious church stands in **West Seneca**, the pilgrimage church called **Fourteen Holy Helpers**, inspired by a vision of fourteen healing saints, mostly from the Eastern Roman Empire. Behind the altar Holy Helpers had a mural devoted to this informal cult. (Like the Greco-Roman gods who had their proclivities, each healer was assigned a body part, whose symbols once hung on the church's back wall.) As was natural for a healing-cult, the church has become associated with a modern-day herbal healer, mistaken in her day for a witch. Like the shaman and the druid, other preservers of ancient traditions, witches and medicine people have been linked unfairly with the outright Satanist, should there truly be such a thing. There was a "powerful strangeness" (in the words of a relative) about Mary Pfeiffer, her past, her life in the domain of the Ebenezer Society, her years at the church, and her own unexplained healings. Her great-granddaughter (now a university professor) remembers helping her collect her "botanicals" in the fields as children played by her "medicine shed" on the lawn by the brook. The Buffalo Medical Society tried to prosecute her for quackery, but to no use. She'd saved too many, and had too many supporters.

3) Let's look at a world-class cathedral, **Lackawanna's** wondrous Renaissance-style **Basilica**. It goes without saying that many of the particulars of classic "sacred space" are embodied in it, designed as it was by Emile Ulrich, an expert in "ecclesiastical architecture." Springs and wells are holy and inspirational to many cultures, and the Basilica will always be linked to the natural gas well that since 1891 has supplied fuel to the Our Lady of Victory institutions. Inspired by a vision of Our Lady herself, Father Baker led a procession to the very spot, buried an image of Our Lady, and told the workmen where to drill. Tremendous difficulties followed, but gas was found at 1,137 feet, a remarkable depth. Constantly associated with miracles during Baker's life and even after his death, the Basilica today is the site of psychic folklore. It's hard to get at. Custodians don't feel free to speak on the record, but it seems safe to say that apparitions and sounds are reported commonly here, particularly after-

A Tour of Haunts

hours. And some vials of blood buried with Father Baker were studied recently when his body was moved within the church. They were still liquid.

4) Though only a quarter-mile from Buffalo's Trinity Episcopal, the intersection at North and Linwood (possibly the first paved road in the US) must have represented the bounds of downtown **Buffalo** in 1854. The First Suburban Church here was on what they called then the Black Rock Road, a parish road going to the canal. Today the spirit of **Episcopal Church of the Ascension** is presumed to be that of its beloved patron Father Broughton, whose image has been seen since his death in various parts of the building. There's also some creepy stuff, behind which is the series of transgressions of a bad priest in more recent decades. What the storytellers don't know (or fail to connect) is that some remodeling was done around 1876 by none other than E. B. Green, so many of whose Buffalo buildings are haunted. The Rectory was designed by Green's stable of architects, and the parish hall (by report) by the ghostly Green himself. Unexplained sounds and electrical effects may be nothing out of the ordinary for an old building, and the reported physical phenomena - including a bat that appeared and struck out over the congregation while a new priest gave his first sermon - could have natural explanations. The matter was convincing enough to others, though. My sources are sure there was some type of religious deliverance or site-blessing done here in the 1970s, largely because of these feelings people could only classify as "bad vibes." It had to be a sign of something.

5) Though built in the 1980s, the **Amherst/Williamsville Synagogue** on Sheridan Drive has been called by local ghosthunters one of the scariest places they have ever seen. This would probably seem a joke to the responsible and accomplished people who attend it during the day; but how many of them ever come back after-hours, in the dark? How many of them wander the undeveloped field by it? This may be the source of the ghostlore, anyway. The Buffalo branch of the Paranormal & Ghost Society had heard the rumors and dug into the matter. They found that three men had been killed by a collapsing wall during the construction of this Synagogue. While the building itself is modern and innovative, the land behind it is another story, an abandoned field,

wooded and undeveloped. Rick Rowe took what he considered to be electrifying photos in the surrounding woods, with faint images too subtle to reproduce here. Others who have visited after midnight report howling sounds and even apparitions, like the image of a man carrying a body. It's become a folklore-focus for sure. It's not one of the fundamentals of my understanding that ghosts can be stalked, surprised, and caught on film, but... Some of these pictures are shocking. Check out the Ghost and Hauntings Research Societies, ghrs.org.

6) At least two churches on the **Tonawanda Reservation** are said to be haunted. This isn't surprising, combining as it does the energy of two traditions. A lot of lore has gathered around the **Baptist Church**. Not only have "mystery lights" (which some take for UFOs) been seen in the vicinity, but a remarkable clear quartz crystal was apparently found right near it, and it seems to have been associated with some prophecy or legend I haven't been able to sort out as of July 2003. Austin Fox (*Church Tales of the Niagara Frontier*) gave 1868 as the year the **Presbyterian Church** was built. It's been remodeled and looks younger than that would make it, but the Seneca operate with the assumption that its core is decades older. The Reverend Asher Wright, for instance, may have transcribed at least part of Seneca prophet Handsome Lake's *Code* in a building on this site, possibly an older version of this one. (The prophet himself died in 1815.) Whatever its age, the building has an illustrious legacy, including a psychic one. Some of the Seneca consider it the most haunted building in Western New York. People who visit the church routinely see and feel things out of the normal. Something raises their hair; something touches them on the arm; something brushes their shoulders, even in the middle of the day; something plays the piano in the dark. This church became legendary as a haunted building. So many thrillseekers from off the Res came here that the Reservation had to recruit security in the 1980s. Once during the Christmas season a dozen-plus members of a choir were getting ready to practice. They heard the doors open and footsteps come down the aisles out of sight behind them. Expecting to be joined by fellow-singers, they kept their eyes on the minister. "Let's wait for them," he said. The footsteps stopped, as if a party was waiting, and the singers turned to look. No one was there. "Well," said the minister, packing up

A Tour of Haunts

with a stiff smile. "I guess we won't practice today."

7) Historian Shirley Cox Husted noted several haunted churches about her own Monroe County. One of the most storied is the former **Mother of Sorrows**, now the National Landmark Paddy Hill Library in Rochester's northeastern burb of **Greece**. By the late 1800s Mother of Sorrows was the focus of Old World-style "miracle" stories, including sourceless footsteps, a ghostly night watchman, and a version of the "vanishing hitchhiker," a little girl-ghost who summons the priest to bless her mother. (The girl vanishes; the apparently healthy mother dies soon after.) 20th century schoolchildren reported wee-hour sounds in the current library: clanging pipes, creaking floors, and the ring of a bell right out of *Macbeth*. Others looked in the windows at night and saw a party of the afterlife. Evidently ghosts from Paddy Hill's graveyard roister in its former church.

8) Speaking of ghosts of churches, **Rochester's** Plymouth Avenue is famous both for ghosts and ghosts of the buildings that held them. Two that used to be here are significant in mystical senses. Plymouth Avenue held the gorgeous Greek Revival home of Leah Fox, whose two psychically gifted sisters virtually gave rise to the religion and the phenomenon of Spiritualism on their 1848 Rochester visit. The majestic **First Spiritualist Church** was also on Plymouth Avenue, and, since Spiritualism is basically a religion of "after-life communications," it would be colloquial to say that this street was the home of ghosts. Alas, during "urban renewal" these two lovely buildings were leveled. One wonders if prejudice on some score could have had anything to do with the choice of route for the expressway. Like the Church of Mormon, another Christian spinoff, Spiritualism has generally been dissed by the mainstream.

9) A tiny brick structure on Pleasant Street is another reputedly haunted **Rochester** church. According to a Halloween, 1993, article in the *Rochester Democrat & Chronicle*, people who live in the neighborhood routinely see ghosts in and about **Our Lady of Victory Church**, particularly in an adjacent courtyard. This little space is grassy and flowered. "The garden-party," they call these apparitions among the white trellises and around the hooded statue of the Virgin Mary. They're especially common in the lush months, July and

August, when the space here is green and in full bloom. They remind people of a merry, faintly chattering garden party, possibly a gathering of late former priests and parishioners. They give most of those who pass them a wondrous, joyous sense of community. They seem so happy. But one neighbor who often took her young grandsons walking with her learned not to lead them past the church when she sensed the presences. The little boys seemed to sense them, too, and didn't like going down the street.

10) The original **Penfield Presbyterian Church** was demolished in 1962. The spot had been a cemetery for early settlers, but in 1826 a church was built over the site, and many bodies were reinterred. About 60 of the unidentified were left. The custom of discarding or burying on top of outdated gravesites was so common in England - said to be the world's most haunted country - that even its greatest literary figure, Shakespeare, framed a curse against it as an epitaph. It's also the inadvertent practice in almost every other Western New York cemetery that's been relocated. Remains are left where they were, undiscovered, or jumbled as they are moved to new sites. It's been no sort of comfort to the modern residents of Penfield, some of whom report seeing many ghosts of the "lost pioneers" in and around the site.

We see that there's some connection between the spooky and the spiritual. One thing that still shocks some people, though, is the idea of a haunted church. "That's one a them contrasequiturs in terms," said one of the people I interviewed. "If God's in, then the spirits are out." *Whose God?* I would have asked if I hadn't asked for it by accosting a stranger. They say the One of the Christians gives people free will. Would it be otherwise with the spirits? Maybe what the Seneca call Him - "Great Spirit" - is a good one. When He's in, there's spirit to go around.

6
Battlefield Haunts

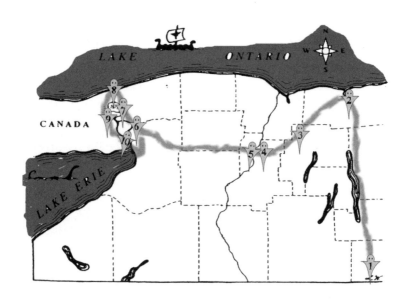

The "haunted battlefield" is another fixture of the paranormal/psychic world-picture. After all, a lot of people got killed there. There have to be "angry spirits" around. Think about that a minute.

If the only connection between a spook and a site was the simple matter of a death, then the emergency rooms of most hospitals would be more haunted than almost any spot of any battlefield. And when have you heard that? But the fact is that clouds of psychic folklore draw to battlefields, and it's the job of this book to report it.

Everyone's heard of Gettysburg, active for one dramatic weekend; but not many people know how hot the Niagara Frontier was during the Colonial Wars. We were the only region in the States to see action all through the War of 1812. Before it was an active, vivid Native American prehistory as well, very little of which we know. A couple of Seneca battlefields (all Seneca victories) are known or suspected in Erie County.

One of the most remarkable aspect of these ancient battlefields is the number of them that could also qualify as "vision-sites," at least to the Native Americans. Is it the energy of a site that draws collective human activity (including conflict) to it, or is it the battle that gathers the spirits? Can't explain it. Let's start with the Revolutionary War battle that broke the dam on the Western New York Iroquois.

1) There weren't many Revolutionary War incidents in Western New York, but a single one made all the difference to the Seneca. Almost three centuries after first European contact the Iroquois Confederacy had suffered no real defeats at the hands of Colonial powers. The Confederacy were major players in the Colonial Wars. In the Revolution they sided with the British, and Iroquois warriors were such a thorn in Yankee sides that General Washington decided to pull it and stamp on it. He ordered General Sullivan to strike against the Western New York homeland of the Seneca, the most formidable Iroquois nation. The pivotal battle was the first. By August 1779 Newtown Point along the Chemung River near **Elmira** had become a rendezvous place for British, Canadian, Tory, and Native American raiders fresh from upstate massacres like Cherry Valley (1778). It was also a natural avenue from the middle states to the Genesee Valley, and everyone knew that through here General Sullivan's army would come. It may have faced an all-star lineup: "White Indian" John Butler, and true ones Cornplanter, Red Jacket, and "the bloody Mohawk" Joseph Brant. Hoping to route the approaching Yanks under their guns, the Seneca and their allies had built a clever fort on a hillside, using natural features to protect their weak points. Sullivan spotted the trap and came at it from other angles. Though Brant ("like a demon of evil") was everywhere in the three-hour battle, rallying his warriors until the bayonet charge that routed them, the game was done at the start. The point became living to fight another day. The Iroquois were marvelous raiders and forest-fighters, but defensive warfare and pitched battle of the European style were alien to them, and General Sullivan's moves shrewdly demanded both. The battle of what would be called **Sullivan's Hill** was anticlimactic - only a few dozen combatants were killed - but the day before it was, so far, the Seneca high-water mark. It was their first real defeat by Colonial powers. Sullivan's Campaign became a 70s Lakers fast-break into the Seneca homeland, burning its ready-to-harvest crops. (You don't need to catch your ene-

A Tour of Haunts

mies if you can starve them.) The battle and its fallout cast a pall of hauntings and other types of lore into the hills, woods and valleys of the whole region, which had to be infested with scouts and raiders of both sides during the period of the campaign. Even today the occasional Revolutionary War-era ghost appears in someone's house, yard, or basement along the likely course of Sullivan's Campaign.

2) **Sodus Bay** was an important harbor on Lake Ontario, and a likely target during the War of 1812. As of June 1813 the expected attack hadn't happened, and people in Sodus must have thought it would never come. Even the garrison sent to protect it had gone back to Geneva. Thus cannon-fire on the morning of the thirteenth was a miserable surprise. Ninety British ships hammered point and harbor and unloaded hundreds of soldiers. Surprised and outgunned, the citizens and local militia rallied and fought, but by the time they had mustered in numbers enough to make a difference, the Brits had achieved their goal: the plundering of the warehouses and the destruction of this site as a launching point for any assault on them. Only one building was left standing on the point, a tavern (some say a fine house) in which an American soldier was dying of his wounds. The retreating Brits didn't have the heart to move Asher Warner from the building in which he sheltered, and left him with some prayers and a jug of water. Some say that as long as it stood this building was haunted by the occasional return of the faint bloody handprints where the valiant Asher tried to raise himself to rejoin the fighting. Bloodstains on the floor, it was said, never came up. Only the burning of the-then Mansion House put an end to the stories about it. But that doesn't explain all the ghosts rumored of this point, including the phantom ships in the harbor and the spectral sailor who objects to any mishandling of his stone. People believe it may be some psychic fallout of the battle.

3) One of the earliest Colonial-era battles between Native North Americans and Europeans took place in July, 1687, at **Ganondagan** in **Victor** (just southeast of Rochester). In the fight to control the fur trade, the French sent the Marquis Denonville and his big, veteran army to attack the Seneca. Opinions vary widely as to the size and savagery of the battle - Denonville's Mohawk allies were said to have been scornful of French reluctance to close with the Seneca. A year

later the Seneca struck back at French possessions in Canada and repaid the blow tenfold, but they suffered badly from the burning of their crops at Ganondagan. That region of Boughton's Hill is widely thought to be haunted. Most of the households around this preserved community have stories of their own. A spectral shaman appears along the roads near the hill, sometimes even trying to enter houses in the guise of a natural effect like a whirlwind of dust or leaves. Maybe this is related to the 1960s discovery of a grave from the 1200s near the hill, that of a woman buried face down and possibly executed as a witch. Some White visitors to the park are affected, some with troubling dreams. Ganondagan was only one of the major towns of a Seneca people who tended to pick up and migrate about every seven years. (They needed to. Their trinity of staple crops - corn, beans, and squash - exhausted the soil.) Ganondagan is frozen in sanctity for inspiring reasons, too. Ganondagan is sacred to all Iroquois as the legendary birthplace of the wondrous Confederacy and home to *Jikonsaseh*, the Peace Queen. Her name means "lynx," but she was also known as "the Mother of Nations," the woman central in the formation of the great League of Five (later Six) Nations we call the Iroquois. Some people believe Ganondagan is a major site for what they call "the earth-force," as if that would explain the proliferation of hauntings and other paranormal effects in the community that surrounds the park. Late Victor historian Sheldon Fisher (who had studied with Seneca scholar Arthur Parker) believed that the Iroquois had kept a crystal, possibly even a crystal skull, at Ganondagan and buried it before Denonville's attack. We don't know what's become of it, though Sheldon also believed that today's Six Nations folk have lost the crystal tradition. Ganondagan today is a New York State Historic Site and a park that welcomes visitors.

4) In 1998 American Rock Salt company started excavating for a 9,000 acre mine at **Hampton's Corners** in the town of Groveland, about six miles from Letchworth State Park. From the start there were environmental protests, particularly over the use of the former mines in the area; but the issue was complicated by the discovery of at least eleven separate burial areas on the site holding the remains of people from Native American cultures. Some burials were only two centuries old, but others dated from 4000 BC, and some may have been 10,000 years old. It was clearly a multicultural

A Tour of Haunts

burying-ground, holding people of many nations. The Native American Graves Repatriation Act - with all its contrapuntal nuances - entered the picture, and all heck broke loose. After numerous protests and lawsuits on many fronts, Seneca leaders came to agreement with mine owners and state officials. The bones - every last scrap of them, in theory - were relocated to nearby portions of the property where they wouldn't be disturbed by the mining operation. The site itself doesn't seem happy. The mine has seen its accidents, and as for the prominent people who made the decision to allow the desecration of burial-ground... Suicides, sadness, ruined careers... Even locals have suffered. Artifacts and bones came up in the work of making the road to the new mine, and a woman who touched the first piece of skull lost her mother, suddenly, the next day. Someone else who took an artifact lost a leg, and many accidents happen on nearby stretches of Routes 5 & 20 where they overlap. A prominent elder from downstate visited and gathered the community. "This is battlefield as well as burying-ground," he said. "Ask permission if you have to pass through." He showed people the areas to avoid, and from which, above all, to keep children. "Kids are susceptible. They'll see things the parents won't." He worked a ceremony to ease the offended spirits and ward off harm to the living innocent, but mercy doesn't seem granted in all quarters. It would be interesting to call up the late motorists and ask them what they saw to make them lose control.

5) One well-known haunt near the spring at Caledonia had been a longtime Seneca torture-post. Hunters learned to be clear of it by sunset, and even into the 1800s the terrible cries came routinely enough that local landowners took their up-for-a-wonder guests out to hear them. Though the **Torture Tree** in the town of **Groveland** is famous only for a single incident - though that one a double - similar rumors attach to this spot two and a half miles south of Geneseo. In this famous episode at the westernmost point of General Sullivan's 1779 campaign the Seneca vented their frustration onto a small party of scouts led by a young Lieutenant starting to make himself a reputation. At the Battle of Freeman's Farm Thomas Boyd's squad of riflemen headed off a British breakthrough and turned Saratoga (1777) into an American victory that may have saved the Revolution. Once on picket duty Boyd surprised a couple guys scouting the wagons and

brought them in singlehanded. They were notorious Tories. ["You have rid the State of the greatest villain(s) in it," wrote General Schuyler when Lt. Rolf Hare and Sgt. Gilbert Newbury swung for their atrocities at Cherry Valley.] Boyd may also have been cursed. (He miserably dumped a loving fiancé, maybe even drawing his sword to back her off in public. "I hope you're cut to pieces by Indians!" she cried.) Refuting his orders at the start of the mission and the advice of his Oneida guide Chief "Hanyerry" during it, Boyd and twenty or so of his men chased a handful of decoys into a formidable ambush. Though the respected "Indian Fighter" Timothy Murphy - collector of his 33rd scalp the night before - and seven others ignored Boyd's orders, made a furious break, and clubbed and hacked their way out, Boyd and the rest dismounted, took cover in a clump of trees, and were killed or disabled in musket-fire from at least 300 Seneca. Boyd and Sgt. Michael Parker were probably grilled by "White Indian" John Butler, his crueller son Walter, and their Mohawk cohorts; then they were handed over to the vengeful Seneca, lashed to an oak, and mutilated beyond belief. Ghastly rumors attached to the site in the nineteenth century, as if shadowy figures returned on occasion to replay the horrid trauma, resounding through the groves and valleys. Why not? Bones, buttons, and weapons were being found here by local kids even after the Civil War. The energy of these reports diminished in the twentieth century, and today local residents claim not to know a thing about them. But recently a massive tree cracked near the Groveland ambush-site and fell on a dead-still day. While in 1842 the men themselves were reinterred with honors in Mt. Hope Cemetery in Rochester, the Boyd-Parker Memorial stands on the south side of Route 20A just east of Cuylerville in Livingston County. Not even a descendant of the original *quercus* - a huge white oak - is standing, but so far as anyone knows, this is where the two men died.

6) Delaware Park and Forest Lawn Cemetery across the expressway have lots of open, pastoral space through which folks in **Buffalo** have walked for generations. For years I've had their reports on file, of faint human images in the distance against the treeline at dawn and twilight. The matter never made sense till I started this chapter. This area was once Judge Granger's farm and the winter campground of American troops during the War of 1812. General Alexander

A Tour of Haunts

˜ ˜ ˜ 49 ˜ ˜ ˜

Smyth - commander of the "Army of the Niagara Frontier"- seemed a soldier afraid to fight. His 4500-man army should have been overwhelming in that time and place, but it retreated from an assault across the upper Niagara. (The other guys fought back!) Smyth delayed the rematch so long that people were more than wondering. The able and memorable General Peter Porter - whose banquet was once interrupted by a British cannonball crashing through his riverside house - called Smyth a coward, and a duel of some sort resulted. Smyth was harsh, though, on others who disliked fighting - or his delay of it. He shot five men for desertion and mutiny and nearly caused a camp rebellion. His awful speeches drove his men to bash their muskets on the trees and fire them in the direction of his tent. Smyth left for Virginia, but he left his army with no choices. They sickened, starved, and froze in the Buffalo winter of 1812-1813. Five to ten a day died and were buried in multiple graves. The Ononadaga limestone that gave **Flint Hill** its name made for hard digging, and most graves were only a foot deep. In the spring of 1813 the bodies were reburied in the sandy ground of the meadow. The plaque at Main and Humboldt honors the spot where 300 American soldiers died. The marker in Delaware Park Meadow tells you where they've rested for almost 200 years. No wonder there are stories.

7) The **Devil's Hole** near **Niagara Falls** is the spot of one of the most famous massacres in Colonial history, one of the most famous battle-and-disaster-sites in the United States. With the French and Indian War the British had won control of the Great Lakes water routes, and thus the rich North American fur trade. The route from the western four Great Lakes to the Atlantic through the St. Lawrence River featured one big portage along the way. (If you don't hear that one coming I can't help you.) The British had hired Native Americans to be porters along the route around the Falls, but when wagons were found to be more efficient, they "downsized" up to two hundred Seneca. Touchy situation. In September 1763 came the Seneca version of a wildcat strike. Twenty-five wagons and fifty English soldiers were virtually wiped out near the Devil's Hole by a single volley, fired from cover by a Seneca force of up to 500. With knife, club, and tomahawk the Longhouse warriors swarmed the wounded, some of whom leaped over the edge into the torrent to sure death. A drummer-boy who did this may have been saved by

a drum-strap that caught on a slopeside tree. A too-small rescue party from Fort Schlosser blundered into more of the same medicine, and dozens of them were killed. Disasters continued into the twentieth century. President McKinley toured Devil's Hole in September 1901 hours before his fateful visit to the Pan-American Expo in Buffalo, and some connect it to a file of ill-omens that preceded his assassination and the file of haunts along his varied stops. On July 1, 1917, the Great Gorge Route Trolley derailed, shooting one car into the howling vortex and fifty passengers to death. Even that may not be the end. Strange sounds, agonized voices, and apparitions of the dead returning to replay their deaths are all reported of this area, one the ghosthunters tell you - perhaps for dramatic effect - to be wary of.

8) Moving up the river on the old portage trail we come to **Fort Niagara**, probably the most famous haunted site in Western New York. (It's one of the handful the national anthologies always mention.) In the colonial wars this region at the American side of the mouth of the Niagara was swept by European, Colonial, and Native American armies, and was the scene of several engagements. In the days when edged weapons - sword, bayonet, and tomahawk - were the deciders in most battles, virtual castles like Niagara could be the keys to regional power and saw serious action in all the Colonial Wars. (You can play beach volleyball on top of what Niagara left of Fort Mississauga in Niagara-on-the-Lake, for instance, virtually powdered long-range from across the river.) Naturally, this fort at the mouth of the Niagara controlled water travel between the Great Lakes, and many generations of fort-builders apparently knew that. The high ground of today's fort had at least twelve earlier ones underneath it before the present one, and authorities vary on what else. (Some mention an ancient Native American fort, and others report the finding of dozens of burned skeletons from the same period, victims of battle, slaughter, sacrifice, or plague.) As you'd gather, the fort's legacy of hauntings is vast. Though the famous six ghosts first mentioned in Samuel Deveaux' 1839 guidebook may be simple folklore, the impression that the fort is plagued with a variety of other effects is strong. TV and radio crews have recorded unexplained images and sound effects at the fort. Most of the fighting in the 1759 siege of Fort Niagara was launched from the western end of what would be today's town of

A Tour of Haunts

∾ ∾ ∾ 51 ∾ ∾ ∾

Youngstown, which would have been quite a dying-ground and features a handful of great haunts today.

9) Through the Canadian city of **Niagara Falls** runs the busy thoroughfare of **Lundy's Lane**. Like "Cemetery Ridge" in Gettysburg that also held a burial ground, it was once busier in another sense. By 1814 the Americans were starting to win the War of 1812. Yankee armies ranged the Canadian side of the Niagara and came into conflict with British-Canadian foes. Around seven on the evening of July 25 the army of General Winfield Scott advanced up a quiet country lane toward the cemetery on the hill. Among the headstones was a battery of British cannon under Canadian Lieutenant General Gordon Drummond. Control of the hill seesawed. Clouds of smoke and night-time fighting made it hard to tell friend from foe. An hour after midnight one of the war's hottest fights ended in an odd double-victory. The British kept the hill, but the Americans carted off the artillery that had been making life so tough for them all around the Falls. Meanwhile, 1700 British, Canadian, American, and Native American fighters lay dead, sometimes in death-clinches or mutual bayonettings. Some were buried where they fell. Others were cremated, and their ashes and bones were buried in pits nearby. The hill is now called "Drummond Hill" after the bold general Sir Gordon, Upper Canada's chief administrator after the war. Although a memorial was set up in the cemetery, the city of Niagara Falls continues its spread over the battlefield from which grim relics still turn up. The site also has its share of ghosts, of which historian Matt Didier and the Ghost Researchers of Ontario have made a fine study. They've taken interesting photographs, as you'd expect at a battlefield-cemetery. Probably the best of the reported apparitions - decades old - are the three ghostly Redcoats spotted moving toward the hill and past the homes on Lundy's Lane near Drummond Memorial Church. Once Ontario's number one tourist site, Lundy's Lane had handfuls of freelance tour guides, grey veterans of the 1814 battle who employed themselves hosting visitors. Since all sides saw Lundy's Lane as a win, a party was guaranteed a happy outcome if the gabbing vets gleaned its nationality.

10) There's always a "rubber" match in a tie, and the third set of Lundy's Lane seems to have been at **Fort Erie**, the bloodiest site in the known history of Canada. In 1814 the

Americans rampaged through Upper Canada and took control of the fort at today's town of Fort Erie. Sir Gordon Drummond tried with all he had to dislodge them. His efforts became a month-long siege, unsuccessful and gruesome. The affair featured cannonball lobbing, seesaw fighting and, at one point, even the unlikely condition of each side controlling a different part of the fort. (The close-quarters settling of that issue had to please Sir Gordon, grimly-admired for his penchant for deciding issues with "cold steel," sword and bayonet.) Today the restored Fort Erie seems to have an ample cast of spooks. Some of them don't crystallize into distinct images. Sometimes all people can sense is that they're spooky and humanlike. Others are recognizable, like one apparition in a high top hat that seems to make no sense in the history of the fort. However, once you get accustomed to the irregularity of most old-time armies - freelance outfits and homejobbed weapons - he doesn't seem that out of place; and who knows why any ghost does what it does? The man in the high hat could be anyone who had a connection to the Fort or the site. One of the most colorful Fort Erie apparitions is a tag-team, a pair of ghosts, one headless, the other handless, wandering the grounds outside the Fort. It had gotten into the folklore that one soldier was giving a shave to another and firmly gripping the razor when a cannonball hit the barber in the mitts at a dodgy moment. The shaver lost both forearms and the shavee lost his head. This seemed like an unlikely story till two bodies were found in a recent excavation, one buried minus forearms and the other lacking a skull.

7
Haunted Highways

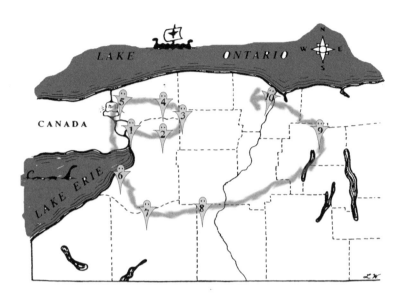

Any stretch of street with a few haunted sites could be on a list of "Haunted Highways," but here we consider ones with an aura, where the sense of distinct spookiness follows a man-made road.

1) Linking two former cemeteries, **Buffalo's North Street** holds a host of hauntings. Even today many hauntings happen in or near the confines of the former Delaware-North burial-ground, roughly bounded by Delaware, North, Irving, and Allen streets. Most of the buildings at the corners of Delaware and North have their stories. Buffalo resident Mark Twain wrote few ghost stories (and none seriously), but two of the handful he finished seem to be set in this area of Buffalo. At the other end of North Street is Symphony Circle and the old Black Rock burying-ground, also a "potter's field" (where the po' fokes gets planted). It turns out that neither cemetery was completely relocated to Forest Lawn when the 1870s move was made. Bones turned up frequently in both neighborhoods. As if we needed graveyards, though, there's so much sacred architecture on the street (including a monumental Classical former Christian-Scientist church) that "spirit" has a ready home.

2) The main complaint in construction-happy **Clarence** seems to be that, as of 2003, every scrap of greenspace is being developed; thus an undeveloped mile-and-a-half stretch of street is a curiosity to begin with. **Delaware Road** is a desolate-looking place. There's almost nothing on either side of it but woods. Kids who've explored them come back with creepy stories, like finding pits full of animal carcasses, as if Satanic sacrifices had taken place. They say cops have set foot in the woods and gone missing; that black cadillacs - driven by "Men In Black" - stalk the road; that cyclists turn down it and vanish; that a spectral young girl approaches a man holding a lantern as if he's waiting for her. This is probably all just folklore. (Missing cops, for instance, would attract quite a bit of attention.) Sources do tell us that there was a suicide on this road, and mysterious lights are reported in the woods just off of it. This area was originally called Westphalia because the settlers came from that part of Germany, and this is what the town of Clarence (in which there still is a West Phalinger Road) was originally going to be called. Clarence is the oldest township in Erie County, and slaves were brought here in the late 1700s and early 1800s to dig ditches to drain the area. Maybe they didn't dig deep enough. The road still floods in the spring. Maybe they're still here. When they died they were simply buried here. Could their spirits be the unexplained lights people still report in the woods on Delaware Road?

3) The **Tonawanda Reservation** has several potentially haunted lanes, the most storied of which could well be **Sandhill Road**, which comes on to the reservation from Indian Falls Road. Sandhill has an illustrious history, which may be what gets the folkloric wagon train rolling. There used to be an old sawmill on the road, and the eminent Seneca leader Ely Parker was born here. At one point about a mile onto the Reservation on Sandhill Road they've seen what they call "changelings." (By the use of this old European term they mean people with animal features, like a fox tail or bear ears, usually thought to be shamans or witches either caught in the act of transformation or careless about the wind-down.) The Iroquois have a vivid fairy lore of their own, and the Little People, too, have been reported on this road, as well as something new I don't want to visualize called "mole people." Off Sandhill Road runs Shanks Road, and more than one person has reported shapeshifters there

A Tour of Haunts

too.

4) We can't forget **Cold Spring Road** in **Lockport** near Desales High School, home to one of the most famous bogies of the northtowns, something they call "The Cold Springs Witch." The folkloric jury is out on what, precisely, she is: witch, ghost, "vanishing hitchhiker," or some other option I haven't considered. Even her precise appearance seems to vary. Sometimes she's a young girl, sometimes a mature woman, sometimes a crone. Prevalent is the sense that she may be associated with the Cold Springs Cemetery. Whatever she is and whatever her point in appearing, there's no doubt that people have reported something on this stretch of road for generations. One of the best reports was given by a woman startled enough by something she drove through on the road to burst into a doctor's office, stammering. The image was stark and womanlike.

5) There are probably "haunted roads" on every reservation. Folklore gives us an explanation for the haunting of **Black Nose Springs Road** on the **Tuscarora Reservation**: that the Iroquois occupants of the land - almost certainly Seneca in those days - killed some White settlers and threw them into the nearby pond. Their pale faces kept appearing just under the surface even years after the event. Massacres keep coming up in the folkloric explanations for hauntings, but real massacres aren't that common or that easy for the historians to forget. If there's any truth to the background of this tale, the event had to happen in the very-late 1700s or early 1800s, unless it was some offshoot of the War of 1812. (Both sides in the war had Native American allies.) As for the ghost stories, though: living witnesses tell us that on certain nights when people drive down the road, unsettling faces appear in their mirrors. Sometimes there are funny sounds on the outside of the car, as if something is either running alongside and tapping it, or has hitched an unlikely ride.

6) Sometimes this aura of a place can be tracked to a single real event, which, in the case of **Angola's Holland Road**, is one of the most horrific accidents that ever took place in Western New York. In the winter of 1867 a train had just left the Angola station on its way to Buffalo when a flaw in a wheel sent a couple cars off the tracks, dangling one of them off a bridge near Holland Road. This had the effect of sand-

wiching the passengers between two blazing wood-stoves that had been at each end of the car. Forty-plus people were burned to death, most of them beyond recognition. Sketches of intelligent human beings reduced to featureless mud-people are sickening, and reminiscent of the lava statues at Pompeii. If it's a ghost impersonating one of these bodies, it could be taken for anything. Maybe that's what's behind the mishmash of campfire-tale folklore here about some sort of faceless old-man bogie they call "the Pigman." There may also be no connection between calamity and codger. "The Pigman" may have been an old butcher fond of mounting the heads of slaughtered swine outside his Holland Road house. (In some stories he wacks all the way and kills a couple children.) Historian Cheryl Delano told me recently that a butcher who happened to live in this area had indeed been shot, possibly killed, probably in the 1950s. Most of the people who recalled the lore of the road for me didn't even know about the train accident. There may even be ceremonies out here (or ghosts of them), since robed gatherings are also reported in the woods and fields off of Holland Road.

7) Some ancient mound-building culture left its trademarks in the sprawling Zoar Valley, but more historic Native Americans - like the Seneca - didn't live in it, considering the area to be haunted. It's no wonder that one of the roads cutting through it should be troubled. The hauntings of **Henrietta Road** in the town of **Ashford** may go back generations. Some of the psychic sights and sounds may have explanations: the crying babies, for instance. (One family on the road had fourteen children, five of whom never made the age of four. The five are buried in a ring around a tree on the road.) One ghost is a boy who wanders the road, dripping, wearing weeds. He seems a true one. Long before her birth, the uncle of one of our interviewees drowned at six, tangled in the vegetation of a pond. A woman who had witnessed the event as a child eventually lost her mind - or did she? - thinking the dead boy still talked to her. Neighbors and motorists spot him wandering this road at night, still in his waterweeds. Another uncle was killed in a motorcycle accident, and this young man is also spotted, apparently walking the road, fulfilling his commitment to come home. One old farmhouse seems a magnet for these spooks. In spells its lights act up on their own.

A Tour of Haunts

8) In other cases the pattern of a spooky road is hardly historic, and you don't have much idea what's going on. **Spring Valley Road** near Route 305 in **Black Creek** (Allegany County) was the scene of a major flap of sightings of something I call the "Black Creek Whodat," an utterly indescribable thing that set the region in a tizzy. Nobody seems to know what it was: a ghost, an albino Bigfoot, an extra-terrestrial.... Something spooked people, roused dogs, dented cabins, and terrified livestock. It may have mutilated animals and left a strange horrible smell in its wake. (The classic Bigfoot is said to be so fiendishly fragrant that in some quarters it's called "The Skunk Ape.") Big white "things" running with "astonishing speed" were spotted in the woods and in car headlights. Hunters scoured the region after them, but the swamp - in which beeping noises and strange lights, fixtures of UFO tales, were rumored - was impenetrable.

9) It may shock you to think that something as big and well-traveled as Interstate **Route 90** could be haunted, but it may be the case with a piece of it. The east-west 90 links a series of cities - Albany, Utica, Syracuse, Rochester and Buffalo - on a stretch of upstate territory about which regional commenters like Arch Merrill and Carl Carmer sensed something otherworldly long before it became a high-speed interstate. As if it were the stroke of a cosmic painter across the map highlighting a band of religious activity, they called it "the Spirit Way." (A suspicious number of countercultural religious movements and communities sprouted or relocated here.) Stretches of the 90 have their own "vanishing hitchhiker," particularly around the Batavia exit. (The State Troopers got some *verrry* interesting reports in the 1970s.) However, some of the most serious spookery happened somewhere east of Rochester during a night-and-day project to route the 90 through ground sacred to the upstate Iroquois. The elders tried everything they could behind the scenes to get the State to listen but it was no good. Finally, they called everyone on the Reservation together. "Don't go out tonight," they said. "We're doing a ceremony to keep the highway from going through. You'll see and hear things you don't want to be around." They did no less than ask the dead to walk. In the words of a witness, "The workers (messed) their pants. Stones were rolling as if people were kicking them." The course of the Thruway had to change, with a bow in it that doesn't show on the big state maps. "The old cul-

tures hang on to that stuff," says Mike Bastine. "This is what keeps us connected to the spirit world. They're here to help us if we need them. As long as we keep looking out for them."

10) If the rumors are true, **Manitou Road** in **Parma**, west of Rochester, is haunted by a frisky demon that scratches at the glass on cars and windows and rushes observers. Historian and author Shirley Cox Husted spent a night in her brother's farmhouse and woke to scratching on the window. Something ugly and terrifying rushed her, only to disappear as it would have struck the glass. She screamed, and the household came running. She'd imagined it, her brother and sister-in-law said, as they said years later when a child was spooked by the same freaky image. Yet when her sister-in-law passed over, her brother, living alone in the house, never raised the shades after dark. Maybe he didn't want to look out the windows. Maybe those who named the street knew something. *Manitou* is an Algonquin word that refers to the fundamental life-force, associated with vitality in natural and supernatural senses. It would indeed be the source of energy for magic.

8
Haunted Theaters

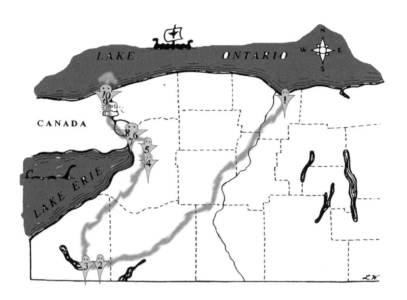

"All the world's a stage," said the Bard. And every stage on the world seems to have its ghost. Our tour of theaters is another admittedly subjective agenda. I could have included them all.

1) One of the civic flowers of the 1920s "**Rochester** Renaissance," The **George Eastman Theater** has, apparently, two resident spooks: a young woman named Catherine whose final performance in life was to throw herself off the balcony; and Mr. Eastman himself, who sometimes appears in his regular seat - number 48. The place may have been the site of a dramatic psychic experience during a performance of Gounod's *Faust*, detailed by Paul Horgan in *Harper's* magazine (April 1936). Cast members held a seance in a Rochester apartment at which some spook announced himself as the haunted soul "Faustus," come back to set the record straight. Maybe to honor the grim play, it promised a demonstration at the company's next performance. On the appointed night, a cross of light appeared on the stage floor and danced like Tinkerbelle in full view of the audience, which included George Eastman. It vanished, and no one knew how it had come to move as it had. The light-room had

been empty, and the crew couldn't explain the miracle.

2) As early as 1875 the folk of **Jamestown** enjoyed fine entertainment. Allen's Opera House (at various locations) presented vaudeville companies known for "general high character of attractions." After an 1881 fire, the last of these structures went up on East Second Street. Lavishly remodeled when it became the Shea's Theater, it stands today. Among the artists who hit its stage: James O'Neill (father of playwright Eugene), W. C. Fields, Lillian Russell, Gypsy Rose Lee, Boris Karloff, John Phillips Sousa, and Ralph Bellamy. Community theater started here in 1920 with "The Players Club," which, in 1936, became the Little Theatre of Jamestown, a non-profit aimed at presenting a play a month, May through September. From this group emerged the most famous person born and raised in Jamestown, at whose 1992 death **Lucille Ball's Little Theatre** was named. From its earliest years there were stories. (A boiler in the basement failed, and while they worked to repair it a director swore he saw a ghost.) Today they say it has a number of haunters, but the one people have seen is a man, as yet unidentified by the folklore. They see him in the boiler room and practice room, even on stage late at night. The Little Theater may or may not have "cold spots," but so often its visitors feel the sudden classic chill associated with ghost appearances and poltergeist displays. The door to the shoe room shuts and locks itself, leaving a guest alone with the stage-footwear. A mysterious prankster has supposedly spoken to children during performances, luring them to cross the stage.

3) Another of **Jamestown's** haunted theaters is just a block away. The vast multi-use **Reginald Lenna Civic Center** envelops the original Palace Theater, a vaudeville and movie house built in 1923. This "theater within a theater" style of remodeling is also that of Sphere supperclub, the former Pfeifer Theater, one of Buffalo's active haunted sites. The theater was renamed after Reginald Lenna ("Le-*nay*"), the local industrialist who gave the first mill of the three-plus for the 1990 renovation. There are several recognizable spooks at "The Reg" (*Rej*), and folklore to accommodate them. They say that a woman, her two children, their nurse, and a Black man were killed in the fire that burned a hotel on this site before the theater stood from its ashes. (There were numerous fires on the site, so... *maybe*.) Sound effects and other psy-

A Tour of Haunts

chic phenomena are said to happen at any time, but ghost sightings come from tours or rehearsals. A woman in white watches performances from the box. A psychic racket seems to start up in the balcony in response to certain songs. The voices of supernatural children have been heard in the dressing-rooms. One of the most distinctive spooks is a tall Black man in top hat and tails. A vanishing little boy toys with tour groups.

4) Every theater has its ghost, and every Roycroft building seems to be haunted, so you'd think the stories about the **Aurora Players Pavilion** would be something. Not necessarily. Unmistakable as a Roycroft building, the deep-green wooden structure in **East Aurora's** Hamlin Park broods beneath so many trees that you can't see it until you're close. You may also have to be on the inside to get the big picture of the ghostlore. I hear that the pavilion's most common guest may be a woman, one who plays with lights and other electrical gadgets, but other specifics have been curiously hard - for a theater - to come by. Actors - like athletes - are notoriously superstitious, and some of these could be afraid that mentioning an experience could bring it back. Town folklore says enough for them. People from the outside spot people on the inside, walking in a dim building that should be empty. Actors report to work on a play and find objects strangely moved over night. Curtains open spontaneously during rehearsals. Other encounters are vivid and personal. People who listen to the scanner a lot hear the town cops talking now and then about lights going on inside the locked empty building. After entering and seeing to the matter of a lamp that turned itself on, one policeman returned to his car and saw another act up. Our confidants heard him say that he didn't want to go in again. When pressed for details the town cops don't enthusiastically confirm this or any story. They don't deny that they get calls about the pavilion.

5) Out of the rubble of the 1894 fire that ravaged most of **Lancaster's** downtown stood the **Lancaster Opera House**. Like many theaters this marvelous, three-story, multiple-service building on Central Avenue is home to a lengthy tradition of haunting. There was a death on the site, that of a caretaker, but folklore blames a mysterious "William" for the poltergeist pranks, regarded as a rite of initiation to new staff. (Custodians have to relock certain doors after someone

somehow unlocks them. Small objects are relocated. Papers on desks are often resorted into chaotic piles. Doors open and close as people watch, sometimes very gently, as if admitting a stealthy invisible presence. The elevator runs itself after hours.) It's a playful poltergeist here, but also a strong one whose feats can be impressive - like the one of July 1988, when a heavy TV set launched itself high in the air across the footlights, came to rest before the first row, and worked as well as ever next time it was plugged in. The resident apparition is "The Lady in Lavendar," one who admires performances from the balcony, then dematerializes.

6) No wonder it would seem spooky. **Buffalo's** 1926 **Shea's Theater** is one of the largest stages in North America, and its Neo-Spanish Baroque environment encourages mystery. Its black marble walls reflect images like Aztec mirrors. Shea's is also illustrious, one of four Louis Comfort Tiffany-designed theaters in the US. As the case with many other reputedly haunted sites, some people who work and volunteer here don't know anything about ghosts. Others have firm impressions of spectral visitors, attributing every curiosity - of which there are many - to the appearance of founder Michael Shea. For some regulars, every slamming door, every blinking light, every unexplained breeze, every feeling of presence is their invisible guest. Why wouldn't he be here? On opening night the living Michael Shea sat among his patrons, tears streaming down his face. This place was in his spirit when he was alive; why wouldn't his spirit be in the place now? At least one ghost is almost certainly that of Michael Shea, since it resembles the portrait of him. And they've seen him recently. During closed rehearsals of *Beauty & the Beast* in the late 1990s there were reports of an "extra" spectator in Mr. Shea's customary balcony seat. In 2000 one woman encountered a very well-dressed man in the same darkened balcony, regarding the restoration work. "Isn't this magnificent?" he said like Gatsby admiring his own mansion. Before she could look at what he was studying and turn back to reply, he had disappeared.

7) In the Prohibition Era, the Town Supper Club - later the Town Casino - was the hippest stop upstate, a Main Street speakeasy and Al Capone's **Buffalo** hangout. It had great food, fine booze, famous entertainers, slinky showgirls, and an aura of intrigue. In recent decades the building has alter-

A Tour of Haunts

nated vacancy and use as several theaters, including Studio Arena and the University of Buffalo's Pfeifer. There's almost too much to write about at 681 Main, now reincarnated as **Sphere** bar and supperclub. It's a building within a building, and samples of the original architecture sprout from the bare old walls through the new. The stage has a cavelike feel, and beneath it passages twist and turn. Tunnels run from the building, reportedly to many other parts of the city. A range of apparitions were reported at the former Pfeifer when I interviewed people in 1996. Sound effects ranged from stalking (like heavy footsteps) to celebrating (like a party in full swing) to staggering (like heavy vault doors slamming). Improbable, if not outright impossible, physical pranks have been played in out-of-the-way places. The spookery has sent employees rushing from the building with lights and appliances running. The occasional "cold spot" affected some people emotionally. (Once a file of people on a tour of the theater passed through one sudden, strange cold spot on a high walkway along the east side. It had to be something to see the dramatic reactions as each one of them went through it.) It's no wonder the former Pfeifer was a folklore-producer. The place is mysterious, especially below-ground. And it's still active if you take the word of the Sphere people.

8) **Buffalo's Allendale** isn't the oldest theater in town, but quality runs here to the roots. Built in 1913 by Leon H. Lempert and Son, the Allendale features a NeoClassical design, one of those "sacred" patterns that tends to attract hauntings. For the Allendale, the Lemperts collaborated with Esenwein and Johnson of Buffalo, who themselves designed the also-haunted Calumet building on Chippewa Street. Isadora Duncan and the "first family" of American theater, the Barrymores - John, Lionel, and Ethel - all appeared here, though we have yet to hear from Drew. Despite its pedigree, the Allendale did a stint in the middle of the 20th century as a triple-X film house. When the 1930's style movie marquee tumbled in 1985, it revealed stained-glass transoms that had been hidden half the century. Only since its recent restoration - and habitation by TOY (Theater of Youth) has the production again lived up to the building. It would be hard to think of one of the Barrymores choosing to come back and haunt a place in Buffalo, but there may be a host of phantom players of lesser fame. The usual run of images at the eye-corners and even full apparitions are reported. Sometimes they're

seen from a long way off during closed rehearsals; someone in the tech booth notes extra actors, even an otherwordly audience. Faint and distant voices are heard frequently, and members of the overnight crew report that stuff happens almost constantly. It starts about midnight, almost as if an alarm goes off, summoning presences to work. This must be one of Buffalo's most haunted buildings.

9) Ghosts are vibrant at **Niagara-on-the-Lake**, and you might expect a theater here to be a knockout. At least two of the three do not disappoint, even providing us with clear and accepted haunters. (This may be the rule in scripts written for Hollywood, but it isn't in research.) The Shaw Festival that started officially in 1962 uses three theaters: the Festival (1973), the Royal George (1915), and the Courthouse. The last one across from the classic clock tower may be the most interesting of the buildings. A jail at its 1840s beginning, the **Courthouse** today is the home of several ventures, including the Chamber of Commerce. It also holds at least one reputed ghost, that of Patrick Boxhill, a beloved comic and character actor who was in Niagara-on-the-Lake in the 1960s and 1970s. Born in England of Edwardian parents, Boxhill was marked by the manners of an earlier age and clung to his own code, no matter what people around him were doing. Even in the disco era he "lived life by different rules," said colleague Christopher Newton with deep admiration. Boxhill died in the later 1970s of sudden but natural causes, and people believe it's he who answers an encore to the Courthouse. They feel him here, anyway. Something will happen, and those who knew him will be sure it was... *Patrick*. What other ghost would be so mannerly?

10) Sparks from a neighboring blacksmith shop set the first Royal George alight, burning it to the ground, probably in the 1920s. One of its neighbors was the Kitchener Theater, a vaudeville house built around the start of the first World War. Bought and renamed, the Kitchener became the second **Royal George Theater**. Sold to Shaw Festival in 1980, the Royal George may be the most atmospheric of **Niagara-on-the-Lake's** three theaters, boasting as it does the most classic stage. This ghost-of-a-building is revisited, they say, by Nancy Kerr, another classic character actor. Born in Saskatchewan, educated in England, and working in Niagara-on-the-Lake about ten years, Nancy Kerr died of

A Tour of Haunts

~ ~ ~ 65 ~ ~ ~

cancer in the early 1980s. She was known as one of those actors who may never have played a large part but who made extraordinary appearances. She was the one you wanted for that small key role, one the audience needed to notice when it doesn't notice that it does. Nancy Kerr always delivered, as she does, on occasion, they say, today. No one can account in any other way for the delicate appearances, the presences they know almost without noticing.

Shaw Festival is a prestigious stage on which many of the world-famous have cut their chops. But the ones who seem to come back here are not the Hamlets and Eliza Doolittles of the world. It's more touching that actors who grew into every play at a single stage are those who burn bright in it when the brief candle is out.

To me the theater is the most traditional of the arts. Jazz musicians seldom play opera. Today's sculptors don't copy Praxiteles, and popular poets love to fancy they flaunt "the establishment." Actors, though, embody tradition. They walk into parts from plays throughout the history of the art; and the Shaw folk have private traditions other than ghosts. When a colleague dear to them dies, they gather, usually in the George, and give tribute. They call up old conversations; they replay scenes in which the actor figured, do the parts as the actor did... And adjourn to the Royal George basement bar and "drink ourselves happy." No wonder actors come back.

9
Haunted Landmarks

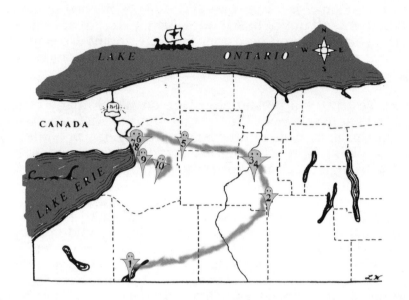

I didn't know how else to classify this one: Really big things that may be haunted. They're so big you might think of some of them as energy-sites, and some are at or near such places. But these spots have to be thought of as hauntings. They're big, they're bad, they're here. And they're also famous.

1) It's hard to find any bit of space that might be considered the haunted node of the **Allegany Reservoir**. (It's big enough to show up on a AAA Road Atlas state map, so it has to qualify as a landmark.) Because of repeated flooding of towns and cities downstream - like Pittsburgh - the Kinzua Dam was authorized in 1963. In the process of backing up the Allegany River and turning a big Southern Tier valley into a lake, it flooded loads of Seneca history. Somewhere under the water that spills into Pennsylvania is the spot of Cornplanter's grave, a simple tree under which the warrior was buried in 1836 at the age of 100. Probably only the Seneca knew which one it was, if it was still standing, but what a tragedy it had to be to them to lose access to it. Cornplanter's village and Handsome Lake's vision-site were here as well, now under water. It's hard for non-Iroquois to appreciate the anguish this caused the Seneca. They protest-

A Tour of Haunts

ed bitterly, but couldn't stop the eventual construction of the dam. All through the cycle of protests, lawsuits, and construction the whole region was a site of massive supernatural lore. Phantom horses, all sorts of legendary Seneca bogies, and even the Great Snake of the Allegany - an archetypal image if ever there was one - were spotted, as if the unrest among the Seneca loosed the zoo of their psychic bogies. Even High Hat, the cannibal-giant in the Abe Lincoln stovepipe, was reported, sometimes by White construction workers. Even today the place is spooky. Salamanca historians tell us that not too long ago the Army Core of Engineers were inspecting the dam from top to bottom, but the divers didn't finish the job underwater. Creepy, shadowy shapes buzzed and drifted around them by the dam wall. Bigger than the divers. The men got spooked, came to the surface, and refused to go back down. Of course the shadow-figures had to be lake sturgeon or muskellunge, which can maybe grow... almost that big.

2) The pioneer settlers of **Dansville** heard a big boom in 1798, and were startled to see a new, mineral-rich spring. Breakout Creek was nothing but a local wonder till 1854 when Rochester businessman Nathaniel Bingham opened The Dansville Water Cure. Hydropathy (one of the crazes of the mid-19th-century) meant baths, showers, wet sheet wrappings, douches, and drinking. Lots. By 1858 Our Home on the Hillside" gained a national reputation under Abolitionist lecturer and publisher Dr. James Caleb Jackson, inventor of "Granula," the first cold breakfast cereal. "Our Home" in Dansville attracted a stable of alternative (for the day) heavy-hitters: Frederick Douglass, Susan B. Anthony, Elizabeth Cady Stanton, Horace Greeley, and Clara Barton (who stayed ten years). The main building burned in June 1882, but three generations of Jacksons ran the new brick facility - the Jackson Sanatorium - through 1914. A short-lived veterans' psych hospital and a series of failed resorts followed. In 1929 came another savior, a pro wrestler, health faddist, publisher, and body builder. Bernarr Macfadden renamed the sanatorium *Macfadden's Physical Culture Hotel*, offered a wide range of treatments and sports, and made it a haunt for the rich and famous. The media-keen McFadden sponsored publicity stunts to celebrate fitness. Named for the cereal that nourished the participants, his annual "Cracked Wheat Derbies" were marathon group hikes to Dansville from far parts like

New York City or Philadelphia. A latter-day Jack LaLanne, McFadden even made a parachute jump on his 81st birthday. After Macfadden's death in 1955, New York City hotelier William Fromcheck opened Bernarr Macfadden's Castle on the Hill as a hotel, but by 1971 the doors again closed. The empty, deteriorating monument nestled into East Hill makes a Gothic scene. It's always had the association with alternative healing and thinking, with which a sense of the numinous often goes. And how the hills must echo at night for those who know its past and study its crumbling present. It's no miracle that this eerie site is one of the most storied in Western New York. So many apparitions are reported here that it's almost useless to describe them, but Buffalo ghost researcher Pete Sexton has taken one of his most impressive pictures here. The property known as **Castle on the Hill** is privately owned - and patrolled. If you trespass, you'll be luckiest if you're caught and prosecuted before you go in. This place is dangerous.

3) About every seven years a terrible flood had devastated the lower Genesee Valley as far back as records go. In the Flood Control Act of 1944 Congress authorized the **Mt. Morris Dam**, built from 1948 to 1951 on top of a thrust-fault across the Genesee River. The biggest concrete dam east of the Mississippi River may be one of the biggest haunts. "The spooks are in the dam," said one of my confidants. "People have seen and heard them." Maybe the legends are due to the men that regional folklore maintains are buried inside the massive dam, like they say of cursed cargo ships. (Park Manager Patricia Hixon discourages this rumor; besides being macabre, bodies inside the concrete would compromise the structure.) It's creepy enough inside any dam, and there are odd and unexplained effects inside the one at Mt. Morris that certainly explain the outbreak of folklore: strange vacuums, odd wind currents, sounds like thunderous doors slamming, and a mysterious fog. Nobody knows the force that makes the swimming pool drop several feet, then surge and almost overflow. Other reports run the gamut of psychic sound and electrical effects. They stand out more when you take into account the inspection and surveillance needed at such a facility. A furtive image in the cavernous distance rises in importance if it might be a saboteur. And the mood of the dam impresses the public. One Halloween night they opened the dam to the public, and the event got crazy on all fronts,

A Tour of Haunts

natural and, I hear, psychic. The accidents and near-accidents at and about the dam are phenomenal. Once six tons of falling rock narrowly missed a truck as it entered, falling just behind it like an electric garage door coming down. Every time one of our confidants visits the dam people report new events that seem to them either psychic or so weird that they have to be paranormal. But don't let that stop you from visiting the dam and the area. The beauty of this site next to Letchworth State Park - the "Grand Canyon of New York" - is breathtaking. Waterfalls, gorges, recreation areas, swimming pools, fishing areas, cabins, walking trails... Visitors are welcome all year at the Dam's sparkling new visitors' center.

4) The only thing that goes on at the **Retsof Salt Mines** now is an operation bagging salt above them. When American Rock Salt Company took over these Livingston County mines, one of their first projects was to close the **Cuylerville** wing. Last used in 1933, it had been nothing but an exhaust shaft since. In the 1990s its tunnels were filled with concrete stem to stern, and there's no point trying to get down there. However, the area may still have a female ghost known as the "Blue Lady of the Mines." An azure mist which, in the moonlight, can be any shape you imagine could be the source of the legends about this famous ghost, seen frequently on the land above the former Retsof - "Foster" backwards - mine. She's been seen enough times underground, though, including recently, and it makes me wonder if the simple explanations are valid. (In the 1980s there was a report of some apparition like her from a man touring the Cuylerville offshoot.) People presume she's the image of a woman, wandering the shafts in search of her husband, lost in one of the many accidents over the years. Some historians believe her tale may have grown around an actual incident at the mine in the early 1900s. The stories about her are varied. Some portray her as an omen of disaster; miners who see her will never make it out. In other tales she's a savior, alerting miners to dangerous situations. In the most common version I hear, she has no mission at all; she's just the mournful apparition of a woman with a lantern whose glow is blue.

5) Most people don't think of something big, bright and lively like an amusement park as a likely haunt, but haunting is a strong local tradition with **Six Flags Darien Lake**. So far I can't think of any reasons for it. Genesee County historians

tell us that before the land's 1964 transformation into an amusement park it was open farmland with a lake, about which no one recalls anything morbid or peculiar. There have been deaths at the park - lightning-strikes, accidents, drownings - but they don't seem out of proportion to the numbers that come here for entertainment of so many types. It doesn't matter; many current and former employees maintain that the park is vigorously haunted, and they should know. Security has to be vigilant at the region's biggest amusement and entertainment park. Most of the warm months, hordes of campers are within walking distance 24-7, and in many stages of celebration; and the park is full of hazards, natural ones like pools and lakes, and titanic man-made ones like roller-coasters and ferris-wheels that could be climbed or damaged. The night crew make good witnesses, and they say they answer many false alarms. It's common for employees to report for duty and find everyone in a stir over something that had just turned itself on, quickly and suddenly, then shut itself off the same way. The bright overhead lights do likewise. There should be no explanation for it, and the mammoth scale of everything at Darien Lake makes these sudden surges especially shocking; it takes a lot of juice to get something started here. And there are the apparitions. The shadows that could be people walking among the still rides have to be pursued, and the staff go on countless wild-goose chases after-hours. One persistent phantom has been that of a shadowy swimmer, breaking into the pool for a few late-night laps. An older gentleman who tragically died had hopped the fence after-hours and must have suffered a heart attack while in the water. Security had gotten so used to the phantom swimmer that it took a little extra time to realize this swimmer was real.

6) The old section of the **The Buffalo Museum of Science** is classic and monumental, seeming to imitate the tone and imagery of an ancient Assyrian temple. Maybe this helps to make it haunted. Sometimes people just get a feeling. Sometimes it's a cold draft or an unexplained smell - perfume or cigarettes. It could be sounds and electrical effects. Whatever it is, mystery is proverbial among the staff. Some say you can sit alone in the main hall at night and hear the empty building murmur. Sometimes the sounds are targeted, even personal: cries from a stairwell, and voices calling the listener's name in many parts of the building. (Caterers ran

A Tour of Haunts

out one night when an invisible woman kept yelling, "Get me out!" and, "I'm locked in.") People also see things: late staffers back at their former posts; persistent, unexplained shadows; even an odd thing they call "sparkle-lights," sometimes caught by the security cameras. Patrons see images of someone behind them in reflective metal or glass surfaces. (Of course, no one is there.) Something visible "passes through" even members of the staff. But the Museum spirits show character. Those on the third floor have a special distaste for Nine-Inch Nails. They'll turn off the blaster or even wreck the CD. Other music calms things on a creepy night. There are darker whispers, something the old staff called "the dark cloud," a plague of tragedies, disasters, even murders, befalling the staff and their families after shrunken heads had been handled. But the Museum spooks can also be comforting. In sad times many staffers have felt caresses on the face or pats on the back, even an ongoing battle between old friends and nasty new spirits, a push-pull into situations that can be dangerous or challenging. Voices, touches, even grabs have warned guards of danger. The building has been blessed at least twice, and purified once with a Native American ritual, which seemed to cool one spell of activity that seemed related to a Native American exhibit (one kind that often seems to be haunted here). Think, though, of the shifting exhibits - mummies, weapons, artifacts, grave-goods - from far parts of the world, some of them mystical and sacred, maybe even cursed. Think of what they have in the closed areas. How would you know the source of any haunting here?

7) The heart-center of our region's biggest city is the octagonal Niagara Square. Its obelisk, fountain, and siting make it, geomantically speaking, a rare accumulator of power, and a logical site for **Buffalo's** most important building. George Dietel and John Wade's highly ornamented **City Hall** features many occult images, and it's done in a style that leaves architects seeking terms. ("Art Deco"; "Eclectic Classicism"; "American Modernism...") Sited above the obelisk of the McKinley Monument, this 1931 building may also be the sort that preserves human psychic energies. The square was the scene of Buffalo's last public execution, that of the three Thayer brothers from the Town of Boston, NY. The brothers seem to have been irreverent types. (They called their oxen "Jesus Christ" and "God Almighty.") They killed their tenant

John Love over a debt and buried him in the woods. Shallowly. (His toes may have been sticking up.) The brothers were soon caught, convicted, sentenced, and led to the budding city's square on June 17, 1825. The cocky Thayers may have presumed the spectators were there to rescue them, as (estimated at 15,000) they could easily have done. The guards were actually worried. But people were just there for a bit of rope-dancing, and, as it dawned on the brothers at the triple gallows, one of them started making a strange sound, a miserable high-pitched keening, maybe imitating pigs being killed. The others took it up. This may have been a ghastly in-joke with the brothers, but the crowd took up the sound for reasons of its own, and the square echoed with the piggy squealing. It was a surreal scene ended only by the brothers' final bucks. The sound is still reported on occasion inside the magnificent City Hall building. Surely it's the elevator-cables; though some think it may be the sound of the Common Council's displeasure at being downsized. Shadowy, vanishing images are reported in the halls of the vast building, and the place may be the producer of other hallucinations. For instance, Buffalo politicians keep doing the same things. It's called perseverance when you keep plugging away and expect things to get better; when you keep doing the same thing and expect them to go differently, they call it...

8) The 17th story clock-tower of **The New York Central Terminal** dominates **Buffalo's** East Side. Designed by New York architects Alfred Fellheimer and Stewart Wagner (known for their work on railroad buildings), the Central Terminal opened on the summer solstice in 1929 and handled 200 passenger trains a day. It hit hard times after the stock market crash, and the proliferation of the automobile gave a fatal hit to the railroad business in Buffalo. Like City Hall, Central Terminal has an odd, megalithic quality, and I can't help but wonder if there might be some astronomical connection between the two. For many a soldier during World War II this was the last look at family, friends, and anything familiar, and the projection of the emotions of human dramas like those could explain some of the feeling here. Only a few years after it was built this monument became a shell, and the domain of thrill-seekers ever since. Neighborhood kids report voices, footsteps, and other typical spooky stuff. (Illicit tourists often hear "phantom footsteps" as if they're being

A Tour of Haunts

stalked through the massive tower-like structure.) Some other folklore is just plain creepy. People claim to stand in naturally lighted rooms, able to see everyone and everything around them, and be shoved, sometimes to the floor, by something invisible. The dreary sub-basements are often flooded, and no matter how many times the basement is drained, the water always comes back, even though people know of no spring beneath it. Some who visited these sections reported "strange reptilian footprints" and bubbles in the water as if an ominous and gigantic bullfrog were beneath. Even the sounds of roaring have come from this area, which sounds a bit like of the UFO-folklore you get on the internet. It's hard to overestimate the Central Terminal's position as a folklore-producer.

9) In 1972 the two-time AFL champion Buffalo Bills readied to abandon War Memorial Stadium, "the old Rockpile" on the city's East side. Work started on mighty Rich Stadium, as it was then named, and they started clearing the former farmland. Soon something seemed rotten in **Orchard Park**. Families living on the edge of the tract noticed things around the house that seemed to them psychic and scary: sinister little pranks; troubled animals; tense families; "energy" spots. Some people felt targeted, even cursed, and got the sense it had something to do with the budding stadium. A tiny graveyard dating from 1820 had been rediscovered in the early going, that of the second owners of the property, the Joseph Sheldon family. It was reverently treated. But Smokes Creek curls through the area of today's **Ralph Wilson Stadium**, and along it had been much Native American habitation. The work had also disturbed their burial ground, and the impression settled that this was the root of the alleged curse. A Seneca rite of healing or blessing was almost certainly done to ease the offended spirits, and grave-goods and contents were reburied. Some Seneca representatives know - or will say - nothing about it. Other Native Americans and some in-the-know Whites are sure some kind of ceremony was done, one that never became public. Both the Bills and the *Buffalo News* have done their best to be helpful, but the matter has been curiously hard to research. In cases like this I usually presume that I haven't talked to the right people or else there's nothing to talk about. In this one, I think either that people who could have said more have simply passed on, or that the matter is sensitive to somebody.

10) It's my book, and I can call **Vidler's** a landmark if I want to. A lot of the life of **East Aurora** has passed through one of the only standing five-and-dimes left in the nation. Oh, for a historic video-cam catching people as they enter Vidler's since its 1930 beginning! What moments of lives it would hold! As would figure, Vidler's has collected a number of ghost stories. Strange sound effects had been heard over the years from the third floor, used only for storage. The noises were like a hard, thin piece of metal being tapped along a wooden panel, as if probing for something. In the mid-1990s someone pulled aside a wall on the third floor and found an old electrician's belt. "Oh, yeah," said the owners, Bob and Ed Vidler. They remembered the electrician who hit the wrong wire and electrocuted himself up there in the 1930s. "They must have hauled the poor fellow out and left his belt." (The Vidlers still have the belt somewhere. No one's reported the sounds since it was moved from its original position.) A brighter tale comes from the back basement retail area. Early one morning in the Christmas season three staffers savored their coffee and waited for the day to start. They noticed a scrap of paper stuck to the bottom of a box of ornaments, a page of music from a 1940s Christmas carol. One lady remembered it dimly and hummed what she could read of it. The others were charmed by the old song, but regretted that they couldn't hear the rest. They were amazed to hear a woman's voice pick up the song, humming the missing verse and even chipping in a few words. A little old lady with bright blue eyes passed between the boxes and smiled to the clerks. They looked at each other, then stopped to think. The store wasn't open yet. They searched, but the lady had vanished.

10
Spooky Communities

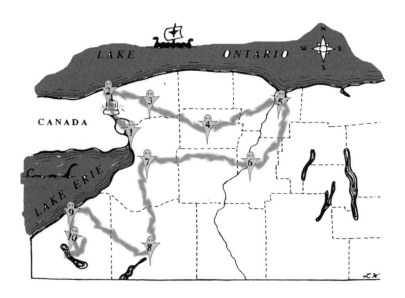

Some communities just give the impression of being haunted. New Orleans, for instance, is a big community that capitalizes on its reputation for ghosts. The Western Door has communities of its own with patterns of hauntings.

1) **Buffalo's** reputation for haunting is not a national one, which makes the ghostlore I pick up all the more convincing. There seems to be a ghost or two on every block in Buffalo. Do a few interviews yourself if you doubt me. In folkloric senses this should be astonishing. We don't have a publicity-machine to push the impression, or a tourist-industry to capitalize on it, so the lore seems natural and homegrown. People are saying what they have heard, and what they think they are seeing. I know too many haunts here to list. Delaware Avenue, for instance: every mansion between Niagara Square and Gates Circle may be haunted. Pick one. I've got stories about half of them. So let's suggest potential reasons for Buffalo's spooks:
History: Relocated cemeteries and old battlefields are under us almost everywhere. Hauntings flower above them. "Remember," said a thoughtful fellow at one of my book signings. "The Erie Indians were wiped out here. Then the

War of 1812. Angry spirit after angry spirit. Not exactly a quiet, cozy town. Whenever you find a Buffalo haunting, it's hard to tell whether it's the spirits of people who lived in the houses, or something from before." Amen.

Natural Energy: One of the few things you can demonstrate in the study of the psychic is that a differing electromagnetism often exists about places that get folklore. The Onondaga flint beneath our whole region might be thought of as another energy-conductor; and the nearness to the radiant natural battery of Niagara Falls should strengthen the case. Father Alphonsus of St. Bonaventure believes that "spooks" (where valid) show themselves in this world where they have free energy to play with. So many of their pranks are electrical in nature, and some of the most famous haunting/poltergeist cases were at sites like the Fox sisters' Hydesville NY cottage, above the natural energy of springs or caverns. Parapsychologist William Roll notices the same pattern in many recent poltergeist cases.

Geomantic ("earth-magic") Energy: Charlotte (NC) geomancer Steve Nelson points out that the hauntings of most cities follow their "energy-lines" (known as *leys*). It's logical to think that spooks in Buffalo would do the same, and they have plenty to pick from. Hauntings saturate the three streets thought to be Buffalo's leys, radiating from Niagara Square: Delaware Avenue; Niagara Street until it bends; and Genesee Street. (The energy of the latter is thought to be diminished and corrupted by the Convention Center cutting it off. The damming of a stream to a city's heart is like blocking an artery in a human's.) Joseph Ellicott's street plan for the original city was probably Masonic - that is, mystical. Frederick Law Olmsted's street-design for the north was likely constructed with feng-shui in mind, if not Native American landscape-mysticism.

Architecture: Ghost stories cluster at sacred buildings. Buffalo is a repository of fine architecture, so much of it done by known sacred architects (Wright, Richardson, Sullivan, Green) or during a period when the tradition was trendy. When I meet this style, it's my rule to expect ghost stories.

Curiosity: Buffalo's soaked with spooks: the by-streets, the cul-de-sacs, the circles, the alleyways... The parks, the waterfront... It started in pioneer days. There isn't a logic behind them. They seem home-grown.

2) To Sir Winston Churchill, **Niagara-on-the-Lake** was "the

A Tour of Haunts

most beautiful village in the world." The town at the mouth of the Niagara looks tame, but if there's another community in Canada so haunted, nobody seems to know of it. Founded after the Revolution by Loyalist veterans, raiders and forest fighters John and Walter Butler, this would have been a bad place to stage a break-in or a holdup till that generation had gone to its rest. The site of a War of 1812 battle, the town was completely burned. Not only is its rebuilt *Fort George* the site of a batch of hauntings - as one would figure of a fort - but the site of a vanished one, Fort Mississauga, is in plain view. Most of the inns and pubs in the village - the *Angel*, the *Kiely*, the *Oban*, the *Buttery* - delight in their ghostly traditions. And these are only the public sites. Ask a few of the locals and you'll see that many of the private homes in the village have psychic lore of a variety of kinds.

3) With the overwhelming presence of the mystical Roycroft, East Aurora might have them all beat when it comes to SPSM (Spooks per square mile). The home of the *Cold Springs Witch* comes in as a startling rival. Soaked in tragedy, **Lockport's** history may be to blame. The first village was the creation of the Erie Canal, every few feet of which represented a life lost. Lockport is famous for some major engineering projects done before the invention of the safety fuse. Many canal workers were killed in premature dynamite explosions, and others were showered with deadly rock-shrapnel. (Visitors to old Lockport reported that it was common to see people with wretched wounds - cracked skulls, bandaged faces, horrible scars.) *Caves* are always associated with mystery and psychic-paranormal lore, and legends gather to those of Lockport, though some of them are man-made. Lockport papers have taken an above-average interest in spooklore and done a fine job preserving this aspect of village legacy. One of the earliest cases they noted was a remarkable Old-World-style spookathon, a one-day poltergeist on *Spalding Street*. One old mansion on a large farm near the escarpment had classic architecture and a legendary haunted stairs. Another family farm house just outside the town was visited by psychic investigators in the 1980s, trying to find the source of its vanishing little girl. One *Strauss Road* farmhouse acted up during the excavation prior to the work on a bypass between Robinson and Upper Mountain Road. (The site had surely been that of Native American settlement.) A ghost may stalk the halls of the *Wyndham Lawn Home for Children*,

formerly Governor Hunt's summer cabin, now a school; sure it is that an owner killed himself here.

4) In the 1980s a man came to the Genesee County historians hoping to find something out that might explain the strange noises he heard in his *South Lyons Street* house. Sure enough, his unquiet home was on the former ground of **Batavia's** first White graveyard. Constant flooding of the Tonawanda Creek washed bones away, and the Pioneer Cemetery was moved in the early 1800s to the oldest extant cemetery in Batavia on Harvester Avenue. Everyone knows they didn't get everything. (As a super market was being built on the same tract they found more remains, some Native American and 7000 years old.) If that doesn't explain Batavia's tendencies to be haunted, its standing as the home of William Morgan, "the murdered Mason," should have some folkloric spillover effect. There are many stray hauntings in the former "capitol" of city-planner Joseph Ellicott after he was nudged out of Buffalo. Ellicott himself could be the invisible guest at his former workplace, the 1801 *Holland Land Company Office*. A character in his best days, Old Joe did lose his mind toward the end, and may have taken his own life not long before the William Morgan mess blew up in 1826. (Born the day after Halloween 1760, Joe Ellicott could have known something sticky was brewing.) A wealthy woman at *Liberty Street and East Main* was so devoted to psychic communications that her home became known as "the seance house." The most dramatic Batavia haunt is probably the *Old Firehall*, which built up a long record of hauntings during its stint as a pub. (Hazardous-duty places like firehouses also pile up hauntings, and before World War One a man was killed in an explosion in this tower, haunted, they say, by his image.) Today the Firehall is home to the Genesee County historical society, and the spookery includes cold spots and a regular apparition on a certain stairs. (Some link it to that ghastly bust of a woman in a shroud, right there as you enter from the east side.) Some folks won't stay here after hours.

5) **Rochester's** reputation for occultism was once so strong that it was called "City of 1,000 Ghosts." The prime source of everyone's impressions is probably the latter-19th century flowering of Spiritualism and the mysterious rappings - the "Rochester Knockings" - that followed the Fox sisters to their stay in that city and even supplanted, in the popular mind,

A Tour of Haunts

the activity from their Hydesville hometown. Before the birth of Spiritualism ghostly rumors hovered about the areas of Rochester's big cemeteries, *Mt. Hope* and *Holy Sepulchre*, and they continue. Folklore about buried treasure, phantom ships, Devil-appearances, and, of course, ghosts hover about the beaches, bays, and harbors of the city's Lake Ontario coastline. *Durand-Eastman Park* along the bay features the avenging spirit "The White Lady of Irondequoit." Rochester's sections of *Corn Hill* and *Paddy Hill* had many mediums in their day, and haunted traditions continue. Some of Rochester's individual hauntings have been so famous that they've made national publications. Some kind of incident at a house on *Hawley Street* made the pages of *Fate* magazine in July, 1955. At the famous *Werner House* (45 Ringle Street), a converted barn, mysterious sound effects were reported throughout the 1930s, seeming to echo a hanging-suicide from 1900. *127 Davis Street* is the site at which beautiful young Tessie Keating knocked one fateful afternoon in 1900, looking for work. Her body was found the next day behind a billboard, and her spirit seems to have driven her murderer to confess. *Plymouth Avenue* was once the major street associated with Spiritualism, holding as it did the first Spiritualist Church and the home in which the Fox sisters held court and "broke" themselves to the world.

6) Settled by Whites a bit earlier than some other places in Western New York, **Mt. Morris** at the head of Letchworth State Park was also heavily occupied by many Native American communities, and my friends in the region consider it a very haunted town. Among some of the locals is the impression that the 1838 *Mills Mansion* has many "guests," possibly because it was built near Seneca burial ground and right on top of the site of a very large burial mound. Two houses west is the site of the former *Main Hotel* - now apartments - where one war veteran reported seeing ghostly images of the Iroquois False Face healers, one of the most powerful presences that could be imagined. Right up the hill near social services is *Oak Grove*, where the Seneca held their council fires. Old growth forest near here has never been touched by the edge of a metal axe, and in the spring the oaks here are said to bleed red. Even non-believers see faint images among the trees. On top of this hill is where Tallchief had his home, and the herbs here could be the remnants of his garden. A former owner tells us that the *Allegiance House*

(now a B&B) was a vivid local haunt, featuring (at least during the 1990s) many harmless psychic events and a cast of former occupants. Ghostlore sprouts in other communities with an underground - Pittsford, Lockport, Buffalo's theater district - and the presence of tunnels under Mt. Morris is worth mentioning. Mt. Morris' were almost certainly pressed into service with the Underground Railroad.

7) Let's give **East Aurora** a fair shake. It may be the most haunted community its size in this part of the state. It may also be that any other community would look that way with a resident collecting every scrap of folklore. The truth probably lies in between. A lot of history happened in a hurry at *Roycroft* at the turn of the 20th century. If you believe in "psychic batteries" - things that influence the development of psychic reports in neighboring areas - the influence of the Roycroft Campus could be significant. There's nothing like this mystical, inspired community of medieval-style buildings in this part of the state, maybe anywhere in the states when all factors are considered. (Whether on the campus or not, every village building associated with Roycroft - like many "Craftsman" homes - has some kind of psychic tale, as does almost every pub in the town.) The village could also have been an ancient battlefield. (Sober historian Orsamus Turner reported bashed bones beneath every basement dug in the original village, as if the region had been a mass prehistoric battle-and-burial-ground.) The spirit and image of a mother who died too young seems to bless her former home on *Paine Street*. Neighboring haunts on *Oakwood Avenue* are the sites of a former funeral home, a 1990's suicide/double homicide, and several other suicides. (Oakwood is flanked by two cemeteries, and I almost made it one of our haunted roads because of the pattern of haunting and calamity on what I call "suicide alley" on my East Aurora ghost walks.) Psychic stories linger about the beloved *Vidler's* 5&10 on Main Street, as well as the theater and its neighboring buildings (including *Fowler's*) on the south side of Main Street, site of a displaced cemetery. (Most of the action here is sound effects from mutual basements and stairways.) Apartment buildings on *Cazenovia Place* and *Prospect Avenue* have ghostly sightings and a few "hard-to-keep-rented" apartments. The village is ringed with reputed haunts in the picturesque hills, including the lovely *Old Orchard Inn*, a handful of churches, and even a haunted *Moose* fraternal lodge at the

A Tour of Haunts

eastern edge of the village.

8) Several theories about ghosts seem fixed in the popular mind: murders, battlefields, Native American burial ground, tragedy... Few seem involved in any of the hauntings of **Ellicottville**, a lovely creekside ski town at the foot of the best mountain in the western part of the state. The spooks of "E'ville" seem the presences of people who loved life here so much that they never wanted to leave. Family homes whose grandparents linger. Old maids who love their houses... too much. Walk the tender streets, Jefferson, Elizabeth, Martha, look under the trees, and imagine the old presences still on their porches. Of course the major streets - Washington, Monroe - have had their fires and disasters. The reputedly haunted *Ellicottville Inn* is on the site of another that completely burned. A recent, questionable suicide may be at the root of rumors at the *Ellicottville Brewing Company*, a former church. Neighborhood tales about one B&B may start with its role as a former funeral home. (Locals nickname it, "the Dead and Breakfast.") *Dina's* fine restaurant was a Masonic meeting hall; maybe that occult tradition in its past explains the occasional poltergeist effects reported by former employees. A handful of psychic incidents are reported in the same long chunk of buildings holding a dentist's office and a bank. An executed murderer may be the source of the top-floor sounds and footsteps in the 1887 *Library* (in the form of a Greek cross). His skeleton was kept there when it was a school. Some apparition that surfaced near the *Train Station* in 1913 was dramatic enough to make the Buffalo papers.

9) East of the village was an impressive fort at a high point called Fort Hill. A pit by it held a mass of jumbled bones, and relics were found all over the area. Other earthworks bracketed the village to the northwest and southwest, and one looks like it could have been on or near today's SUNY Fredonia campus. Something was clearly going on here before the colonials arrived; but the likely positions of these old monuments seem well removed from the scenes of most of the hauntings, so your guess is as good as mine why **Fredonia** gets so many people talking about ghosts. As we've seen earlier in this book, the *White Inn* has its tradition of haunting, as does the *Opera House*, like all theaters. Graduated actors testify that two theaters in the same building on the SUNY Fredonia campus - the *Marvel* and the

Bartlett - may act up when witchy or sinister plays (like *Macbeth*) are produced. Fredonia's fabled *Igoe Hall* may act up any time. At one home near *Temple Place* - that of a late, beloved doctor - a life of devotion has become an afterlife. (Phantom footsteps are still heard approaching the phone whenever it rings late at night. The MD son, still in the same house, jokes, "I have to beat Dad to the phone.") The building they call Old Main at *One Temple Place* - former home of a boarding school and SUNY Fredonia - was the scene of a horrible early 1900s fire, involving many tragic deaths. A young woman still running back for her engagement ring and a faithful caretaker - Phineas Moore - who died trying to save others may be among the apparitions. Few of Fredonia's haunted sites have ever been publicized, but the town seems saturated with haunts. Many graduates of SUNY Fredonia have stories about psychic phenomena in some apartment they rented or visited in the village. Fredonia hosts delightful Victorian-themed ghost tours in horse-drawn carriages, usually in the fall, and these are not to be missed. Ask the Chamber of Commerce when you're in town.

10) As the home of Spiritualism, **Lily Dale** (in Cassadaga) could be termed "spook central," since, in the shorthand, the faith founded upon Swedenborg, Andrew Jackson Davis, and the Fox Sisters is a religion of spooks. Though just as capable as anyone else of having a laugh, folks in "the Dale" don't think of it that way. To them, the spirits of our dead are capable of speaking to us, sometimes even showing themselves, in any place and time. When you decide to be open, or when you visit someone else who is a professional "door-opener" - a medium - some of them will probably come to you. At other times, they may get frisky. While every spot of the earth is considered "haunted" in this logic (the spot is irrelevant), some of the Lily Dale B&B's and other buildings are known to have "company," as the regulars call it. There's certainly a mood here. People have asked me why I don't write up and lead a ghost walk of Lily Dale. I always answer that there would be so many great hauntings on the first block that it would take two hours to get through it. A side problem with such a ghost walk would be that every resident of the village would be at least as qualified as I am to lead it. Even more so. (They could tell you what the ghosts are trying to say, for God's sake!)

Ways of the Spirit

The Marker at *Kanadesaga*
Photo by Jean Taradena

(Note the naturally-formed image of a human face in the foliage to the upper left of the marker at this Seneca burial mound in Geneva. Jean's seventh-great grandfather was a chief here, Old Smoke. The image reminds her of a famous portrait of Red Jacket, who also spent plenty of time at this village.)

A
Vision-Places

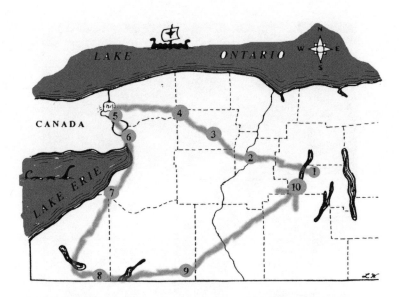

We know the basic seven life-processes, defining qualities to all that lives: breathing, eating, reproducing... Maybe one thing that makes people different from animals is an eighth component, the urge to observe something spiritual.

All known human - societies have felt this mystical-spiritual-religious impulse. Most honored it by commemorating special places that were thought to enhance the spiritual experience: holy sites, where it was easier to reach the divine. Spirit-places.

The ancient Egyptians believed that no site could be truly sacred if it wasn't already sacred to an earlier people. The pattern holds in most parts of the world, and almost every place special to the Seneca of Western New York was special to somebody among the cultures who had preceded them. And to these sites layered with spiritual significance, supernatural lore gathers, including that of all modern types. Often the witnesses of supposed paranormal events know nothing of the area's significance, which makes you think they may have been responding to something at the place that would enhance the visionary moment, and that this

WAYS of the SPIRIT

~ ~ ~ 85 ~ ~ ~

energy is almost surely still there. But let that be. "Vision-Places" is a chapter about sites themselves known or presumed to have been sacred to the Native Americans.

1) Let's start in the Western Finger Lakes near **Middlesex** and a monument so big it still seems to some a natural feature. What I call **The Great Circle-henge** wasn't even "discovered" until 1980 when someone at the Yates County Soil and Water Conservation Service was going over aerial photographs from 1974. Only on foot can you reach the earthen arc in Clark's Gully, and you may not spot it even when you're close. The diameter of the full circle would have been a thousand meters. What you can see from the ground - the northern third - is about 35 feet across and five high. Maybe the henge was never finished, but only a full study could tell. It may be only a few centuries old; but the Seneca questioned knew nothing about it. Who made it? Some folks who like explanations simple say it was made by a meteor-strike. The Hopewell-style stonework right by it makes others think the arc is man-made. We may have lost our chance to tell. Farming activity has greatly eroded the circle since World War II. But this had to be a mighty meeting-site for some ancient culture, maybe several. Maybe it was the Stonehenge of the prehistoric Finger Lakes. Monuments this big are special, and yet this one's slipped through the cracks of history. Can you imagine what went on dead-center of this circle?

2) On the west side of the river by **Mt. Morris** is the legendary **Squakie Hill**, cut in two by the road that comes into Letchworth State Park through the Mt. Morris entrance. A Seneca village was here in historic times, and probably others long before them. Seneca old-timers reported that whoever lived in the area spoke a different language. The hill's name could come from that of the Kahquas (the Neutral Nation), rumored once to have lived there. It could also come from that of the Sac, or Sioux (the Fox nation); people of that origin were said to have settled here as prisoners, which could also account for this region's occult legacy. (Magic is almost always a resort of society's underdogs - slaves, captives, and the dispossessed.) Remains and earthworks of very ancient cultures have also been found in the area. Just to the northwest of the Seneca village was burial ground, and bones and weapons were being found here near the surface into the 1900s. The Seneca always considered Squakie Hill an

occult and mystical site, particularly as this land was being taken from them in stages. Squakie Hill was the scene of festivals of the White Dog which some Whites were allowed to see. It was also the site of the farewell dance to the Genesee Valley the Seneca performed as they prepared to leave it. One specific figure associated with the hill was the Seneca medicine man John Jemison, murdered here in the early nineteenth century. The Seneca believed he came back to haunt the place, and if you visit Squakie Hill on the right nights, who knows what you might see?

3) "The Place of the Great Hearing," the Seneca called this bend of the Tonawanda Creek in **Batavia** and its life-giving spring. They met here annually, some say, for councils. Who knows what it was to cultures before them? Even modest fountains and wells have always been sacred, and many of the world's great prophecy-sites - like Lourdes and Delphi - were near some such natural feature. But sure it is that this was a council-site. With the guidance of the spirits, many grave and visionary decisions would have been made here at the convergence of ancient footpaths bringing people from the four directions. (As is the case elsewhere in Western New York, these trails became significant modern roads, today's Routes 5, 63, 98, and 33.) The spring served generations of Native Americans and colonial settlers, and it was visible into the 1980s on the lawn of a Main Street church across from the Holland Land Company office, long-time home of the Genesee County Historical Society. A sculptor even offered to make a bronze statue to honor the tradition but, alas! the church behind it was demolished and the fountain paved over. Even the plaque was taken in 1998 and now rests at the Holland Land Office Museum. All it says on it is **Indian Springs**, but why leave it where it was? It would only call attention to what we've lost. Maybe if you come by the garage and towing service after hours and stand long enough on the black top you can hear something otherworldly of your own. Maybe we ought to open this one up again, and see if the sculptor's offer still holds.

4) The place on the **Tonawanda Reservation** we call **Spirit Lake** is the last existing remnant of Tonawanda Lake, 12,000 years old. Sometimes also called "Divers' Lake," this body of water on the Tonawanda Creek was the site of an ancient chert-mining operation that may have been as old as the lake.

Archaeologists went there for years and could often find projectile points and tools made from the dark gray rock out in the open. Part of the reason they call it "Spirit Lake" is because the images of the ancients were so often reported here. Some say Spirit Lake was the haunt of the Great Horned Serpent so strong in Iroquois mythology - which means it was a place of Big Spirit. The Little People are reported here, too, as if the place were sacred to them. This piece of land is privately owned now, and I can't advise you just to show up. Find out exactly where it is on your own and write to the owners for permission to visit. Don't bother them if you don't hear back. This area has been trashed by somebody, possibly kids who used to party there, possibly just people looking for someplace to dump their trash. It takes away most of the atmosphere.

5) **Niagara Falls** is packed with vision-sites. One of them is an island just below the Great Falls, joined to the city by a small bridge. We call it **Goat Island** because an early settler kept goats there. It's surprisingly young as an island, only a couple thousand years old, a heartbeat in geologic time. (The Falls themselves are only twelve to fifty thousand years old.) To the Iroquois this was Turtle Island, named for their image of the world as a great body resting on the back of a primal turtle. From that we judge that it was sacred to them as an *omphalos*, a world-navel. At its western edge are three small islands nicknamed the Three Sisters, the furthest of them only 300 yards from Horseshoe Falls. Iroquois shamans no doubt prayed on Turtle Island, sacrificing food and other items to the Great Spirit of the Thunder-Waters. They used it as a burial site for their warriors. However, even today people sense some sort of presence about all these islands: feelings of energy and anticipation, and also sometimes dread. Two people who knew nothing about the past of these islands heard an eerie moaning while crossing Goat Island at night. No other people were on the island.

6) Franklin LaVoie tells us that old **Buffalo's** traditional sledding-hill, West Ferry Street (from Delaware down to Linwood) is a leg of one of the city's biggest oddities, a geological structure startlingly like that of Jerusalem. It's a big limestone outcrop shaped like a Y with a fountain at its base. [Its three points in Buffalo are Canisius High School (Delaware & West Ferry); Symphony Circle (North &

Richmond); and the Armory/City Honors High School on Best Street - all areas, by the way, said to have haunts.] The key to this formation is the natural fountain we call the **Cold Spring** where Ferry meets Main - part of today's Route 5 - one of the heaviest intersections of ancient North America. Route 5 was a major east-west trackway across the continent, and the spring at Main and Ferry would have been a rendezvous-point, and a fork in the trail. (Supreme Seneca orator Red Jacket was a regular at the corner tavern; and a young man who would become 13th US president - Millard Fillmore - took his first job as a teacher at a school that once stood here.) When thinking of the Cold Spring Franklin remembers a phrase from the *I-ching*, "to cross the great water." It's a metaphor for the irrevocable choice to accept an undertaking that will be a challenge. For generations of Native Americans, the Cold Spring was such a deciding-place. The spring is now buried under streets and houses at the southeast corner of Main and Ferry.

7) On the **Cattaraugus Reservation** near Lake Erie is **Burning Springs**, one of the handful of known earthworks intact in Western New York. From one way of looking at it there should be nothing remarkable about this mound. Western New York used to be littered with these things. They couldn't all have been major vision-sites, and prehistory doesn't give us much by which to judge what was. On the other hand, for societies whose only means of travel was by foot, vision-sites had to be close to where people lived. Maybe the presence of the vision-site was one reason for settling near it. And there are so few of these earthworks left that we don't get many chances to visit sites we know were ancient, sacred, and ceremonial. And Burning Springs could be special. It was doubtless named because of oil or natural gas nearby that could be lit. (One of our confidants remembers visiting the place as a boy and setting the bubbles alight with matches.) If conditions were different at any time in the past, could it have been lit on a grander scale? What a spectacle that would have made during the visionary ceremony! So you might find your medicine here just by imagining it. We remind you, though, that this site is on private land, accessible only by a logging road, and at least a mile from the nearest paved road. It's also part of a sovereign nation. Don't come out here joyriding without the permission of the Seneca Nation, specifically those on the Cattaraugus Reservation.

8) Sometimes names for things tell you what people found when they got there. **Kiantone** means "The Planted Fields." When the Seneca arrived, somebody had been here before them, maybe long before, and the area just south of Jamestown became important in legend. A natural spring here was sacred to the old and the ailing, and the great Seneca chief Cornplanter (1736-1836) brought his war parties here before and after campaigns, which almost all went well for the old warhorse. But it wasn't only Native Americans who noticed it. In the craze of seances that swept America after the Fox sisters' 1848 debut, Kiantone blacksmith John Chase became convinced that the **Spiritual Spring** held the power to cure all ills. A Kiantone team of adventurers dowsed with a witch-hazel wand, bored fifty feet into the earth, and came up with their healing springs, which soon became a source of income. The water was boiled down and the residue - a white powder - sold. Samples of the water were sent to the leading Spiritualists in the East. This spring became the focus of the neo-Spiritualist Kiantone community, beginning in 1852 and fading through the 1870s. Whether or not this was the spring sacred to Cornplanter, the spirit around Kiantone Creek is high. A Kiantone resident heard a fumbling at the side of his house and found a strange woman sleep-walking. A New England medium, she'd been driving nearby when some mood hit her, threw her into trance, and aimed her car toward the site of old Harmonia. Glowing stones, spectral Indians, and fireballs hurtling up and down the creek figure in the recent folklore. As far as we can gather, the spring is just about obliterated now, having been the spot at which the Kiantone community dug their tunnel, now covered with a Hobbit-like door. It would be a fearful thing to enter. You can probably visit the site if you ask directions and mind your manners. This, too, is on private land.

9) Let's ride down Rt. 16 a few miles south of **Olean**. The Native Americans seem to have had their own *feng-shui* based on a sensitivity to natural features. At certain places the Great Spirit was recognized, and **Rock City** must be one of them. It's the world's largest known deposit of quartz conglomerate, an energy-rock used in ancient monuments and a great natural conductor of electricity. This chunk of it took form 276 million years ago during the Carboniferous Period, fell 40,000 feet, became the floor of an ancient ocean, and shot to its present point 2300 feet into the sky when the

Appalachians were made. Today Rock City is visited by thousands a year, a natural sorcery-garden whose rocky columns weep white quartz tears as if they held imprisoned Merlins. As with the tors of England, you might suspect that man had a hand in it; but it's natural processes that have cracked and curled these rocks into fantastic shapes and distinctive, monumental features. "The Twin Rocks" make a natural arch 50 feet high and may have been a multicultural gathering-place to Native Americans for thousands of years. A big flat stone at its highest place we call "Signal Rock," since a fire set here could be seen all the way to Holland, NY, forty miles off. There are signs that countless such fires were set here. And another wonder exists, a rough, ancient stone staircase down a narrow fissure between two rocks. Once, probably, it went all the way to the bottom. This was surely human-made, but the culture behind it is a mystery.

10) We end our circuit of vision-places with the daddy of them all, **The Great Hill** by **Canandaigua Lake**, birth-place of the Seneca people. (The Seneca call themselves *Nundawaono* - "Great Hill Folk.") I wish we could be sure which one of the hills at the base of Canandaigua Lake it is. Some historians are convinced it's Bare Hill, where, in legend, a great snake killed all a village, only to be defeated by a pair of special children (guided by the Great Spirit) who became the ancestors of all the Seneca. (In its death throes the big snake knocked down all the trees on Bare Hill, accounting for its name.) Others (including Seneca historian George Abrams) believed it was South Hill at the foot of Canandaigua Lake, and most of our Seneca contacts go with him. Western Door old-timers like my late friends Sheldon Fisher and Rodger Sweetland would have told you that it wasn't named in any book. After long study of the legends and probably some communing of his own, the great Seneca scholar Arthur Parker seems to have decided that it was Parrish Hill near Naples, high over the valley that was the legendary birthplace of the Senecas. I lean to this one, since it's where Parker made his cottage near the end of his days. Wherever it is, this hill is the holy of holies to the Seneca, the site of their national creation-myth. It's probably fine with them that it's still mysterious. I'm not sure I'd tell you if I knew for sure. Go on your own little vision-quest if you like. Drive the roads around the lake; hang out in the hills awhile, and see what you feel. You'll have all the answer you need.

B
Around Spirit Way

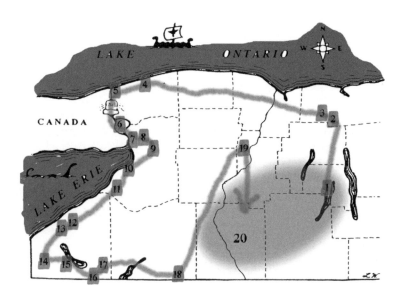

You can doubt the ghosts, UFOs and critters reported in Western New York. Lots of testimony, not much evidence. You can't deny a historic pattern about Western New York, the tendency to start and attract religions - religious cults, communities, and centers. If we don't grow our own, we draw them from somewhere else.

Though regarded as the birthplace of religions, Jerusalem has nothing on us. As I see it, the Holy Land had two hits - big ones, admittedly - but that was a long time ago. Western New York has been a lot more active. It's the birthplace of the two most successful modern religions, Spiritualism and the Church of Mormon, and spots here are still holy to them. In fact, our region was so proverbial as a zone of religions and revivals that nineteenth-century people gave it nicknames like "the Burned-over District." (This seemed to imply that so many revivals had swept the area that any human spirit capable of catching the fire of holy inspiration was already charred or burning out.) Sensing a still-active syndrome, twentieth-century writers like Carl Carmer and Arch Merrill popularized the term, "the Spirit Way."

1) Let's start our tour where it all started for the Spirit Way. Jemima Wilkinson was a pretty, dark-haired Rhode Island schoolgirl who seemed to die of illness in 1776. She was still for hours. At midnight she stood and spoke with a different voice, inspired with the Spirit of "the Lord of Hosts" to reveal the messages of God. No longer Jemima Wilkinson, she was "the Universal Friend of Mankind whom the mouth of the Lord hath named." The following Sunday under a tree at the Meeting House in Cumberland, the core of a sect was formed that walked half a century with her. "The Publick Universal Friend" rode her rolling revival through Pennsylvania, southern New York, and Connecticut with her two "apocalyptic witnesses," James Parker channeling the Old Testament Elijah, and Sarah Richards, doing likewise for the prophet Daniel ("now operating in the female line"). Jemima made some mistakes. Like many cult-pioneers, she had ideas about sex and preached a fundamental, ascetic Christianity. (In private, she may have been more flexible. Word has it that she was more than once interrupted in close circumstances with rich male benefactors.) Her attempts to convert "the savages" (Iroquois) were the stuff of farce. The Friend even traveled about in a splendid coach with the letters "P. U. F." blazoned on the sides. Her harshest critics presume Jemima's reception of the Holy Spirit was a career decision start to end, and that "The Publick Universal Friend" was just one of the historic freaks of the Burned-over District. But her **New Jerusalem** on the Seneca Lake (near today's **Penn Yan**) thrived in grand style, and Jemima was honored and loved in her community. When in 1819 Jemima Wilkinson passed into that long rest for the second time - this one for good - two male parishioners laid "The Publick Universal Friend" to rest in the woods with no monument to mark her peace. These days the land is private around here, and you better ask in town and make a few calls if you feel like sightseeing.

2) Supernaturalism has never really left the West, but the Industrial Revolution and the Age of Reason had most serious-minded people disclaiming it, all but the sober style of mainstream Christianity. Events in a Wayne County hamlet got some people re-admitting that science didn't know it all. The now-vanished **Hydesville** near Newark was a village of peppermint farmers when, in 1848, the Fox family moved into a cottage with a ghostly reputation. Mysterious knocking sounds inside the walls seemed to follow the two

teenaged Fox sisters, launching them into fame as mediums and causing a wave of spirit-communication that became a new religion. Based on the idea that "the spirits" could be studied like anything else, a new religion started declaring itself almost as soon as the sisters went public. A few years after its birth **Spiritualism** boasted two million disciples, among them many of the western world's most prominent people. The psychic events at the root of the matter are controversial, and most people base their judgments of the Fox sisters on beliefs they have in place already of what may be possible. All I can ask you is to make up your mind from the original reports about the Fox sisters, not just the rhetoric of their interpreters. You can see a monument to the birthplace of Spiritualism in the former Hydesville, but the cottage is long gone. (It was moved to Lily Dale in 1915 and burned in 1956. There's an empty space on a circle where it stood.) You can certainly breathe the atmosphere, though, and the fit among you could jog to our next spot. As you do, remember that a cycle that started a few miles southeast of Rochester still affects this world's ideas about the next.

3) Born in 1805 among the wooded hills and still-mysterious stone ruins of central Vermont, Joseph Smith was ten when his family came to **Palmyra**. In 1827 he found... something in a cave in Hill Cumorah, and a star was born. Farm lad Smith told an epic tale of prophecy, war, treasure, ancient American civilizations, and a book written in gold. Smith's band of converts moved westward from home to home, persecuted across the country, and not disposed to turn the cheek. Near the end of his life, Smith (on a white charger) and his five-thousand-man legion nearly joined battle with the Illinois state militia. At Smith's 1844 assassination the budding faith moved to Utah's Great Basin. The cycle is quirky, but there's nothing to be mocked in the success of the **Church of the Latter Day Saints**, who practically own Utah and do missionary good around the world. A few things about Prophet Smith make him interesting from occult vantages. He was a dowser, a psychic, a visionary, and a crystal-gazer. He was fascinated with Masonic regalia and symbolism, and the wife of murdered Mason William Morgan became one of his own. Masonic ideology and hierarchical structure were used in forming the Mormon order, and it's possible that old mystical influences - like alchemy, hermeticism, and maybe even ritual magic - entered the development of Smith. Here on

Cumorah Hill there's a major complex of monuments, and you'll have no trouble finding it when you're anywhere near Palmyra. Even Smith's sacred grove has walking-paths and meditation-stations. Never forget that this is Bethlehem to one of the world's most successful young religions.

4) A sudden spiritual awakening in 1992 set Taiwanese Texan Hon-Ming Chen making bold predictions. He said God would show Himself on cable TV in 1998, and then materialize - looking much like Chen - on a Texas lawn. When that didn't happen, Chen clarified his meaning. ("God did appear, but people don't have the concept to see God because they are limited to the three dimensions.") He lost some followers but continued to call himself the reincarnation of the father of Jesus, which he modestly proclaimed to mean Christ's earthly father Joseph. And the predictions kept coming. The man the papers call a "UFO cult leader" foresaw a nuclear holocaust in 1999, and divine UFOs evacuating believers to the safety of the Great Lakes. (The group has shown photos of what appeared to be chemtrails and declared they were the signs of God's UFOs.) His Way of Truth sect - which mixes Buddhism, Christianity, and flying saucers - moved **God's Salvation Church** to Spirit Way, and 30 of his 160 followers came with him. Their choice of Lake Ontario was apparently a mystical one; Chen's group believes God uses the lake as a way-station for souls and considers the whole region a spiritual magnet. They've made no waves in nearby **Lockport**, except for walking everywhere they go in white cowboy hats. The kids go to public schools, and the parents are involved in the community. We "just want to live a normal life," Chen said. (Yeah, him and Michael Jackson.) As it may be, but from here he sounds like a prime tenant of Spirit Way. If you doubt that he's in historic company, wait till you meet the Millerites.

5) Though only half a century old, **Our Lady of Fatima** shrine in **Youngstown** is a world-class spiritual destination dedicated to the visions "the beautiful lady" gave three children in Portugal. Hundreds of thousands of visitors a year come to commune and take in the eye-popping marvels, like the "Avenue of Saints" (a hundred statues made in Italy) and a huge outdoor rosary. The ten-ton statue of Our Lady of Fatima on the high dome of the chapel is done in a contour of the Northern Hemisphere. There's extensive use of marble

at this 35-acre site whose undoubtedly geomantic (sacred) layout from the air reminds us of Versailles. Why is it here? The surface explanation is that Walter and Helen Ciurczak prayed for healing, were healed, and donated land to the Church; the two Barnabite Fathers who conceived Fatima were in Buffalo by coincidence. Inspired volunteers did the rest. But I go back to the ideas of Carmer and Merrill. Other than posing a rare devotion in the population of Western New York that makes them support this and other religious isms, I can only class Fatima as one more of the highway markers of the energy-zone we call Spirit Way.

6) In September 1825 a grand parade in Buffalo welcomed the new owner of **Grand Island**. A lawyer and the editor of an important paper, Mordecai Noah of New York City was a sociable, strongly-built man. As an ambassador for the young United States he'd arranged some kind of deal that ended the war with the Barbary Pirates. No one knows why he thought of Grand Island as the capitol of **Ararat**, his new Israel; but there was more to him than meets the eye. Rumor holds that Noah was a Mason with powerful patrons. (George Washington came to his parents' wedding, and his rapid rise in life seemed suspicious.) Noah may have stood for a Cabala-cult whose deep mystical tradition he hoped to make the constitution of the new state. Though his proclamation to the Jewish people announced an asylum in a "fruitful and happy country," where their rights and religion would be respected, none of them bit. Noah also thought the Native Americans descendants of the Lost Tribe, and he planned to bring them, too, into the Jewish fold. (You'd need Mel Brooks to bring that one to life.) A day or so after the parade Noah himself went back to New York, and nothing came of the venture. Unless you want to tour Grand Island and imagine Noah's never-to-be kingdom, the only thing to see is his cornerstone at the Erie County Historical Society in Buffalo.

7) Father Nelson Henry Baker (1841-1936) was the force behind one of the most prominent sacred buildings on the Western Door. **Lackawanna's Our Lady of Victory Basilica** fits all the profiles of "sacred space":
1) *Sacred geometry* (It was designed by Emile Ulrich, an expert in "ecclesiastical architecture.")
2) *Earth-energies* (Baker found a gas well after a vision.)
3) *Astronomical alignment* (Most churches are oriented to the

compass directions, and this one was a monument on the horizon.)

One of the greatest humanitarians who ever lived, the soon-to-be-sainted Baker is the focus of legends, including elaborate "miracle" tales. (Healings, blessings, interventions, controlling the weather, even besting the Devil.) Angels - or somebody - have been heard playing the Basilica organ at night. One thing is sure: Father Baker built a whole chunk of Lackawanna, and most of the buildings are still standing.

8) **West Seneca's Ebenezer Society** was another of those communities that might have gone anywhere but ended up on Spirit Way. It started in medieval Germany, where some of its members felt that the Lutheran Church had left its roots. Its dissenters had a revival in 1817; a carpenter named Christian Metz took "The Community of True Inspiration" to a new land. The community of Eben-Ezer ("The Stone of Help") settled in three villages by an ancient wood on the former Seneca Reservation. These thrifty, hard-working farmers kept to themselves, which is probably well. Like the early Mormons, they were into pre-Spiritualist occult practices that would have troubled their Christian neighbors, like channeling (speaking for spirits). In each community, one or several individuals served as virtual mediums. By the later 1850's the Lord called the Ebenezers again. Their thousand souls moved to "Amana," their new home in Iowa. Their descendants are there yet. Today West Seneca treasures the Ebenezer legacy, and you can still catch a little of the old feel in the hamlet named for them.

9) **East Aurora** was already a state of mind, but when **Roycroft** got here we knew what to call it. Freethinking founder Elbert Green Hubbard (1856-1915) was a speaker, an author, a journalist, a publisher, a philosopher, an early Feminist, and a Victorian longhair. Founded as a printing operation in 1895, Roycroft became a world-famous Arts and Crafts Movement community. Possibly a Spiritualist and early psychical researcher, surely a Rosicrucian, Hubbard attracted a community heavily made up of Universalists, Christian Scientists, Rosicrucians, and Theosophists. Hubbard left plenty of what I call "time bombs" - symbols waiting to be understood - at this medieval-like campus:

a) *Magna Mater*, Katherine Maltwood's mystical sculpture behind the Elbert Hubbard museum on Oakwood Avenue.

b) The occult *Red Face on the Roycroft Chapel* (today's Town Hall) on Main Street.
c) The flat-topped pyramid of the *Ruskin Room*, site of so many ghost stories.
d) The nearly isosceles triangle of the *three towers*: the Ruskin Room, the rectangular Cornell Cooperative Center's tower, and the circular one at the Chapel.
e) The Egyptianate *slanting arches* at many places in the Inn. Ones you can't see are hidden in the structure of the south wing, the hotel part.
f) Note the *sacred images* in the Salon's murals, and the mystical *roses* in the Inn's stained glass.
Drop into the Gift Shop and get a look at the Rosicrucian-style poster advertising the first issue of the Philistine, Hubbard's career-long magazine. There's so much else to say about Roycroft that few people see it as it was, a community inspired by spiritual philosophy that ended up on Spirit Way.

10) **Eden** old timers thought a suicide here was really a murder and called the old farmhouse on Sandrock Road "the seance house" because people came here to talk to spirits. Once you were on that ridge anytime in the 1980s you knew something was up. (Could it have been those gigantic metal and canvas soccer balls inspired by Buckminster Fuller's geodesic domes? One ended up storing wood, and another soared over the hot tub.) It's still hard to tell whether man came to mountain because of the energy it had, or whether man brought energy with him. Let's start with the man, Dan Winter, a polymath with a grasp of physics, music, computers, crystallography, and languages. A slim, calm, denimed fellow (born 1952), Dan impressed most of the people he met as a genius, though not many of them could tell you what he was talking about. One thing was sure, though: for 17 years **Crystal Hill** was a meeting ground for the "New Age." A virtual commune, a spiritual center with an organic farm ("a learning center experiment in collective bio-harmony"), Crystal Hill nurtured body, mind, and soul. Guests and boarders spilled into the barn, then a garden of tents in the high meadow from which you could see Lake Erie. Authors strolled past grazing sheep and bounced ideas with local hippies. Crystal Hill's legendary organic Thanksgivings pulled dozens of alternates into evenings of the highest spirit. It also did some hard research, including some astonishing experiments with ESP and psychokinesis (mind-over-matter). One

witness saw people make a rock totter in a fishbowl just by staring at it. Before his mid-1990s relocation to Asheville, NC, and his teaching/learning academy *Sangraal* (Holy Grail), Dan's inspiration seemed to be the image of the dodecahedron. Computer graphics supported his idea that this many-sided crystal embodied the principles of the universe, the earth, and human life. There may be places where they all meet, but my mind was never one of them due to Dan's tutelage. Dan teaches around the world these days, and some folks think the energy is gone from Crystal Hill, now a private horse farm. But Crystal Hill's reach has yet to be measured. Crystal Hill seeded Western New York with folk who can lead others to their own spirituality.

11) Keep south until you get to **North Collins**, and let me know once you've figured it what to make of the legendary "Father John." Born in northern Spain, probably in 1895, Juan Jesus Alvarez came to the US in 1913 and studied for the priesthood. He was a preaching Franciscan friar when he was offended by something, possibly the Church's sanctioning of "gambling" (Bingo), and had his split with the Church of Rome. The people of North Collins built him one of his own, the **Church of the Sacred Heart of Mary**. He was ordained a deacon and priest in the Episcopal Church, which cares lovingly for his congregation today. For half a century this robed longhair was "the Monk" of North Collins, an eccentric so saintly he was inspiring. Like classic saints, his effect on animals was miraculous. Like classic saints, he had been seen in two places at one time. He may also have had psychokinetic powers, mostly relating to the symbols of the Church. (He could read Bibles in unfamiliar languages, light altar-candles with a look, and play holy music on the organ he'd never studied... in a pitch-black church.) What the eye-witnesses tell you about Father John - healing, psychic abilities, and other traits commonly rumored of the saints - puts Father Baker to shame. What the Episcopalians who studied him have to say is buried in the archives. The church and the grave of Father John are both right out in the open; but other wonders will stay hidden. Marvel at the wonder we had on Spirit Way, a man through whom Spirit flowed.

12) If Hydesville was Spiritualism's Bethlehem, the still-thriving **Lily Dale** is its Jerusalem. The White settlers came to the outlet of Cassadaga Lake in 1809, and the first public

building was surely a tavern. In the 1890s what would become "The Lily Dale Free Assembly of Spiritualists" was one of the first communities in the world to be fully electrified. It had energy of other types. Possibly because of the prehistoric monuments - earthworks and roads - found about the lake, the impression entered the folklore that this had been a "conflict-free" zone for many societies, maybe even a multicultural religious site. Even before Spiritualism Lily Dale hosted a series of eclectic associations, and many famous people have spoken here in the last two centuries. Susan B. Anthony came at a time when her message was too radical for other places. Roycroft's Elbert Hubbard talked here when he became a little too on-the-edge for Chautauqua, and in the 1980s and '90s Deepak Chopra, Wayne Dyer, and John Edward followed in Hub's footsteps. The Fox sisters' original cottage was moved here in 1915 and destroyed by fire in 1956. There's a space on the circle where it used to be; but there's a lot else to see. Go to Lily Dale any time. It's one-stop shopping for the meditative. Fall, winter, and spring are entrancing; but in the summers 'the Dale' comes to life. Hike the groves or the woody shrine, Inspiration Stump. Walk the labyrinth of low bushes designed by Vermont (now Glastonbury) teacher and dowser Sig Lonegren. Attend a seminar or visit a medium. Hang out by the Karma Cafe and watch a day pass. Take your journal to any of the shrines about the grounds, or look over the lake. Lily Dale was made to nurture moments.

13) Under a gumbo of mid-nineteenth century Spiritualist-style influences, a minister took up community-building and landed in **Brocton** in the spring of 1868. Thomas Lake Harris (1823-1906) bought 2,000 acres of farmland, started building a huge Italian villa-style mansion, and set a pretty group of lords and ladies to work in the fields. The **Brotherhood of the New Life** held up to a hundred people, most of them high rollers who virtually begged Harris to take their estates and set them to work toward spiritual perfection. Besides a con man, Harris was the most prominent "trance poet" of his day, dictating verse for hours and delivering epic-length poems about humanity, the heavens, and the dawning of the New Age. He taught practices like "Divine Respiration" - precise breathing - to promote spirituality on earth. In some form and location the "The Use" (as its residents called it) thrived almost forty years (1861-1900). But Harris' treatment

of its members could be rough, and in the early 1880s one of them sued Harris for return of his "investment" in the New Life and eventually won. With his third (trophy) wife Harris founded another collective near Santa Rosa, California. The Brocton site eventually reverted to a community member, and became a forerunner of the vineyard business so famous in the lakeshore region. Privately owned, "Vinecliff Farms" survives in good shape today.

14) Ordained a minister by the Apostolic Church of England and sensing a crisis in the human body and spirit, E. Crosby Monroe (1880-1961) retired from business in 1942 and bought three farms outside his native **Sherman**. "Whosoever will may come," was the motto of the **Shiloh** community. Hoping to create an environment to rehabilitate humankind, it welcomed all with "bodily and spiritual" needs... but they had to work. First came a dairy farm, then a bakery and butcher shop. By the mid-1940s the trucks marked SHILOH rolled through Southern Tier towns. By the 1960s Shiloh's 50 folks were active in civic projects, taking over the local phone service and handling emergency calls 24-7. A virtual commune whose meals were shared, Shiloh became a trust whose profits were used for humanitarian purposes. Local folk were still suspicious. Word spread that Shiloh's "brainwashed" citizens were ex-cons and winos that had deified "Father Monroe." (Secretaries did follow the founder night and day, recording his words as if for someday's Scripture.) Monroe was succeeded as trustee by his son, who held his post only a year till his 1962 death in a small-plane crash. Under his successor the enterprise grew into wholesale food distribution that served stores around the nation. Soon Shiloh the business needed a more central location. By 1969 they had set up in Arkansas as the Church of Shiloh, where they are today.

15) Take a jog west to Lily Dale's more proper sister. Ohio inventor Lewis Miller and Methodist Episcopal minister John Heyl Vincent sensed a hunger in the human spirit and wondered what they could do about it. In 1873 they took a boat ride on Lake Chautauqua and envisioned an ideal esthetic community to begin addressing it. Their summer artistic-educational program became perennial, and through its reading club, correspondence courses, and famous speakers, Chautauqua became a household word. Their choice of site may have been easy from inspirational standpoints.

Supernatural folklore, aboriginal earthworks, and an ancient road may suggest this part of the lake as a zone with energy of some sort. Today the **Chautauqua Institution** is 225-acre lakeside collection of contemporary homes, condos, hotels, B&B's, shops, meeting halls, and 1200 Victorian cottages. The community's resident population is about 400; in the summer, 150,000 people may visit. Chautauqua is among the world's elite retreats, intellectual and altruistic rather than simply trendy. Chautauqua's guests, performers, and speakers have been by all sensible standards, at the top. It's not unusual to hang out here on a summer afternoon, get a haunting sense of familiarity about someone you spot, and realize he or she is someone famous. Chautauqua's founding point was to reach beyond any one religion, but its aura of sanctity is undeniable. Chautauqua's temple-like buildings remind us of sacred cities like Athens and Jerusalem. This is one place on Spirit Way where the energy went mainstream.

16) Shortly after the Fox sisters' 1848 rappings, the Spiritualist family of **Kiantone** blacksmith John Chase had the revelation that their valley had once been inhabited by "the Kiantonians," a sophisticated ancient race. A host of mystics took up the cause. Minister and medium John Murray Spear envisioned "noble temples, great universities, and stately halls of art," in **Harmonia**, a model city based on universal brotherhood. A band of followers and a small campus of multicolored octagonal cottages materialized along the Kiantone Creek. Willow trees (for a basket-weaving business) and berry bushes (for a money crop) were planted all over their ridge. The robed citizens of Harmonia held frequent midnight festivals. (Over 5,000 people attended one in the late 1850s.) In 1858 their great convention made the New York City papers, but the mystical energy that drew them faded by 1870. The rainbow campus decomposed slowly across the next century. The willows and berry bushes are all that remain, troubling the modern residents hoping to put the land about them to use. One oddity remains. Since Spear's spirit-guides told him that the site had been the center of an ancient civilization, the folk of Harmonia were always digging for something, either a vast treasure, a source of mystical power, or even signs of the web-footers. They made a strange tunnel in their hill. Wide enough for two people to walk abreast, it went 150 feet back and down like a stairs. (Today it's fearful, snake-infested, and private, and the

"Lord of the Rings"-style door to it is locked. Keep out.)

17) Calvin Kline (1920-1999) was the proverbial "rocket scientist," a computer man who'd worked for NASA. In midlife he was called to found the **Religious Society of Families** at **Oak Knoll** on his Chautauqua County farm near **Frewsburg**. He changed his name to "Calvin of Oakknoll." He claimed to sympathize with Humanists who think the universe is natural, not Godly, and that humanity should look to itself to solve its problems. Calvin offered himself as a solution. Oakknoll's folk were granola-crunchers, living life without fossil fuels or processed foods. (Calvin could name only a handful of members when he tried to get a religious tax exemption, and not many of them were admitting it a few years later.) Calvin also believed that people should "self-destruct" at seventy, possibly to save world resources they were no longer producing. All this we presume. The historians don't know what moved the man, and his code didn't come out at his trial. Yes, trial. Calvin hated hunting, and once sued the state Department of Environmental Conservation for permitting it. (Possibly related to it was Calvin's habit of shooting his neighbor's dogs, doubtless sensing them part of the predatory process.) In 1980 a Jamestown barkeeper out hunting crossed Calvin's land. The spat might have been a duel, but the DA didn't agree that the hunter's shotgun was raised when Calvin's bullet struck. Calvin got fifteen-to-life. The farm is now privately owned, and Calvin didn't leave much to look at anyway... But this was one Spirit Way original, a recent one nipped in the bud.

18) While you're this far south on the Spirit Way you can't miss a swing through **Olean** and **St. Bonaventure University**. While "Bonny" has the rep of a party school and isn't exactly what I'd call haunted, this campus by the river is invested with generations of sanctity, and I think of it as quite a vision-site. First off, one small brick structure out in plain sight seems to have been the subject of a couple of healings. This is the Shrine of St. Therese, set up by a group of seminarians in 1925. The great modern mystic Thomas Merton often prayed before this shrine and came to several of his visions here at Bonny. One of them (maybe in a grotto) seems to have sealed his decision to undertake religious studies. In search of inspiration, Merton used to walk into the hills from the campus, and he's associated with "the Heart of

the Mountain," a natural clearing on a slope, shaped like its name. The students, people say, go there to party; but it may have been the scene of another of Merton's visions, possibly the one that made him leave the world and become a monk. This is wide-open in sight of the campus, but it's a hike.

19) Just west of the Genesee is a tiny village once home to another set of Spirit Way diehards. The Second Reformation of Scotland (1638-49) came to the valley in 1815. By 1823 a congregation set up in **York**, and by 1886 they were 200 souls. But the **Covenanters** didn't aim for converts; they clung to old practices. They refused to pay taxes, vote, or fight in wars. They swore allegiance to no government but Jesus Christ, used no musical instruments, and sang no hymns in church, only psalms, thinking God's Bible gave people all the words they needed. They went to extremes to keep Sunday free from labor, doing double duty on Saturday, if needed, even walking to church so their horses could keep Sabbath with rest. They didn't accept members of secret societies (like Freemasons) and strictly enforced their code. (They handed out cards on Saturday to people in good standing. Only those with cards could take communion on Sunday.) Young people had to leave the group to join society, and the Covenanters' last service was in 1931. Later in the decade their church was torn down, but its tower was saved for the town hall. All that lasts of the Covenanters, it kept time with stunning accuracy, a testament to their passion for true telling.

20) There's nothing left to see, but a couple Spirit Way founding-members are worth envisioning as you curl into the Finger Lakes. The 19th century's greatest American evangelist **Charles Grandison Finney** (1792-1875) did most of his work in Western New York, maybe even giving the Burned-over District its name. **Millerism** was another national movement whose base was Western New York. Biblical "interpreter" William Miller (1782-1849) thought Christ was on the way, and his thousands of followers ("Millerites") got ready. The brothers **Fowler** [Orson Squire (1809-1887?) and Lorenzo Niles (1811-1896)] were the American popularizers of Phrenology (head-reading) Nothing's left of their Cohocton home, but architecture may be their lasting legacy. The octagonal homes they advocated became the rage. Mark Twain retired to such an eight-sided study in Elmira, and others on Spirit Way still stand, most said to be haunted.

tHe X-pLaCes

"X-PLACES," DIGITAL IMAGE BY CHRISTOPHER JANIGA

A
THE X-ZONES

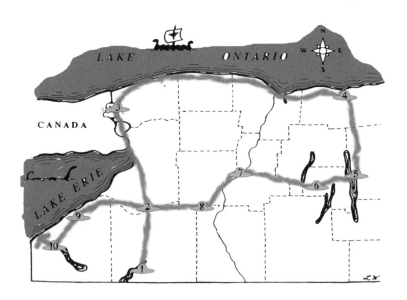

There's the old "traveling salesman/farmer's daughter" joke I first remember hearing as a kid in a tent. Here goes.

The only place for the traveling salesman to shelter for the night is in a barn with the farmer's nubile daughter. The farmer pulls her aside for words of caution and a fruity code by which to call for help in the night. "Yell, *Apples*! if he tries to (kid-word-for-sexual-practice) you..." (Hereafter, *KWFSP*.) "Yell, *Peaches*! if he tries to (*KWFSP*) you. And if he tries to (*KWFSP*) you, yell, *Pears*!" Of course, the girl calls, "Fruit salad!"

It's probably funny only to a ten-year-old; but I use it to illustrate the irrational combination of items that characterizes paranormal folklore. Maybe it's just the way my mind works; but whatever zoological credibility I attach to reports of Bigfoot or South-Bay Bessie (the Lake Erie serpent) involves keeping them separate as categories. (Ghosts are seen *here*, ancient mystery-ruins were *there*, witches hang out in *that* swamp, UFOs buzz *that* hill...) Ghosts seems to stay put at individual buildings, sometimes across centuries; but in broader senses that's not the way psychic folklore usually works. There's a clustering-effect about sites, often areas big enough to be shaped by geology, counterintuitively lumping almost all the genres: mystery monsters, UFOs, ghosts, archaeological curiosities... This turns my attention to the spots themselves at which some nameless energy makes the folkloric imagination cry out, "Fruit salad!" Western New York has a striking number of these "fruit salad" zones, areas of general weirdness. Here are some in which you might want to watch your step.

1) Let's start at the foot of a major upstate UFO-zone. It may be no miracle that one year the edgy Gravity Games made its course the road barreling down from **Allegany State Park** into Salamanca. This huge, hilly, wooded region is one of a number of weirdosities. Several strange stones have been found in the region, including one that appeared to be a "slaughter-stone," a sacrificial object that would have been virtually unheard-of in the Northeast Woodlands; another marked stone that Harvard's Barry Fell (author of *America, BC*) considered to be the memorial of a Celtic King named "Zari"; and, from an ancient burial mound, a copper plate inscribed with the image of an elephant (an animal not native to the Americas in 12,000 years). An ancient stone fort is still here atop a hill called "Old Baldy," and some historians think it was built by a mystery-culture. The "Witch Lights" of Iroquois folklore are reported of an area between the two lakes, Bay State Hill. Ghosts are seen on the trails of the park, sometimes in the images of old settlers, sometimes hunters, hikers, and runners. This park is also the site of Bigfoot reports, UFOs, MIBs ("men in black"), a mystery cat, and even some humanoid amphibian like the creature from the Black Lagoon. Then the folklore gets wild. (A godly giant white bear. Giant furniture in a cave that the government bulldozed shut and fenced off.) Maybe the Seneca knew best. To them this was a region of magic and mystery where anything otherworldly was likely - an "X-Zone," in other words. Don't be afraid of it, though. Just don't feed the bears.

2) A saucer-ride north drops you off in **Zoar Valley Park**, which seems to be another zone of everything. 35 miles south of Buffalo, Zoar Valley is formed by two branches of the Cattaraugus Creek that flows northwest through Gowanda and the Cattaraugus Reservation and empties into Lake Erie at Irving. Some people are spooked by the valley; they say it

tHe X-pLaCes

hums at night, as if it held some vast natural force. They talk about how hard it is to build roads through it that last. They talk about hunters who go missing in the valley. (One who made it out swears to this day that he shot at a UFO right above him.) They talk about lost hikers. (It took a full day for a massive search to find some lost campers recently; they said they'd gone so far into the wild park following other hikers who just... disappeared.) Things spooky are often also spiritual, and in the late 1960s the Valley was hyped all over the country as "hippie heaven" through underground papers. The park's visionary reputation may be partly due to the legacy of these hundreds who camped here as long as weather let them. Yet most of it preceded them by centuries. Ancient earthworks once here may indicate an unknown cultural influence in the area, and there were rumors of oddities surrounding the mounds when they stood: lights, ghosts, other curious effects. There should be; these works are often elaborate graves. Zoar Valley has a number of natural wonders and is a prime focus of Seneca lore, including prominent witch-and-sorcerer tales. (In one still-visible crack in a cliff-wall a wizard was reputed to dwell, and a seminal fairy-tale, the origin-story of the "Dark Dance," also seems set in Zoar Valley.) The notion of an unsettling occultism about the area lasted into Euroamerican settlement. The lore of the valley features folkloric disaster tales, witchcraft, and a macabre curse - crab-claw hands - afflicting the male members of a family because of some evil deed in its past.

3) Scoot north to what they call **The Niagara Corridor**, a stubby north-south brushstroke on the map that overlaps the Niagara River. This mighty wet thoroughfare must have been significant to the old-timers, because ancient forts were reported on every high point on both sides of the river. Somebody was fighting somebody, but the historians don't have much to say about this warlike activity, its scope, its scale, or its players. Its root, of course, is the giant battery of Niagara Falls, one of the world's major power-centers and shrine-sites. Franklin LaVoie points out how transformative waterfalls tend to be, providing people an emotional bath, an experience that symbolizes a turning page. However, this is a famous UFO zone, one of the grand ones in the nation. It would seem that the UFOs have some fascination with the river, the Falls, or the power plants. Weird lights were reported at critical junctures in the local power grid during the

famous East Coast blackout of 1965. And there's more. Very unusual human skeletons were found on the Buffalo side of the river near Fort Porter. Some in the Northeastern UFO Organization suspect that Ivan Sanderson's theory of underwater UFO "bases" could be right on track. People actually report UFOs rising from and entering the lake, presumably connected to two deep depressions at Lake Ontario's western end, joined by a long narrow trough.

4) Make one of those high-speed right-angle turns that are so easy in your UFO. Like Niagara-on-the-Lake, **Sodus Bay** is at the head of another of those north-south UFO-corridors, a channel from Lake Ontario through Seneca Lake. Though less famous than its eastern cousin, it was the scene of a pair of major evening sightings in August and October 1966. People in this part of the state saw a fierce, brilliant light in the sky that flashed red, green, and white over the region, hovered for 30 minutes over spots, and finally headed out over Lake Ontario. Sodus is also known as a bay haunted with phantom ships from the War of 1812. The point itself is the subject of a couple of good ghost stories, as are nearby communities. This may also be a zone of ancient mystery. The famous artifact I call "the Sodus Bay Spearhead" (see *Spirits*) was found in the water a few feet into this bay. On display with the Wayne County Museum in the courthouse at Lyons, many authorities consider it a medieval Scandinavian artifact. How it got here is the story; but in the deep folklore of the area, the Native Americans referred to a mystery community, possibly of Europeans, on the southern shores of Lake Ontario. (Early settlers found the marks of iron axes on trees, and the evidence of the rings indicated they were made well before 1492.) Old maps seem to suggest the same thing, and "fringe" historians like Barry Fell believed in the existence of an ancient trade network in the Great Lakes, even a European colony in Canada straight across the Ontario from Sodus. That would have been an afternoon canoe-ride for a Viking. Strange, elaborate rock-carvings near Peterborough may confirm Fell's theory.

5) In a flash you're heading south and hearing "the **Seneca Lake** Guns," a loud, rare, and apparently natural curiosity for which there's still no confident theory. (Arthur Parker tells us the Iroquois refer to "underwater drums" to explain a similar effect in Cayuga Lake.) Residents have claimed for

a long time that big unknown shapes have been seen in their slim glacial lake. The most persuasive serpent-siting is from a hot summer afternoon in 1900. Passengers on a side-wheel steamer noticed a big object 400 yards or so ahead. It was about twenty-five feet long, and they thought it was a boat till it turned its head and flashed a mouthful of wicked teeth. Eventually boat caught beastie with a paddlewheel, knocking passengers off their feet and killing the critter. They tried to haul it in, but its tail slipped through a noose and slid into the 600-foot deep lake. Several prominent citizens of Geneva (including the police commissioner and the manager of the phone company) reported all this to the *Rochester Herald*. A geologist gave us the best description of the beast: a triangular four-foot head, a long mouthful of sperm-whale like teeth, a horny turtle-like skin, a creamy belly, and fishy lidless eyes. He suggested it might be a *clidastes*, a type of extinct water-lizard.

6) The **Western Finger Lakes** is a zone of ancient mysteries, particularly near Penn Yan. One queer, massive formation of stone ramparts and causeways was named "Bluff Point" after the high point (800') between the fork of Keuka Lake upon which it rested. It was dismantled in the 1930s and its stones used to build the Wagner mansion. However, it was studied on behalf of the *National Geographic* in 1898. ("The strangest work known in anthropology," wrote Dr. Samuel H. Wright of it.) On another high place within signal-fire distance ten miles north of it was the huge ring-fort "Fort Hill," just a bit more like the usual ruins in the region. One of the most astonishing in the world is "the Great Circle-Henge," right round the corner in Middlesex. It could certainly seem that a mystery-culture was active here long ago, and maybe even a mystery-race. A conical burial mound by Keuka Lake disgorged human skeletons in the early 1800's, many of which a Penn Yan doctor found were seven-footers. Rumors of ghosts, curiosities, and buried treasure abounded here in the nineteenth century. Penn Yan was also the place Jemima Wilkinson, "the Publick Universal Friend," picked for her inspired community. Some think she may have known of its power. Her ghost, "The Grey Lady" of the woods and lakes, may have appeared frequently into the twentieth century, rescuing children and guiding lost hikers to safety.

7) Draw a circle on the map a few miles around the point at

which the Genesee hits the head of Letchworth State Park. Include **Cuylerville** and **Mt. Morris**. What you have is a memorable zone of psychic activity, much of it related to its prehistoric past. Historic, haunted, and artifact-strewn Squakie Hill is within this zone, as is the haunted Dam at Mt. Morris, the troubled burying-ground outside the old Retsof Salt Mines and, beneath it, their spooky "Blue Lady." A strange incident from 1807 seems isolated but worth mentioning: a creepy wailing coming from the low sky above the Genesee Flats each night for several weeks, dependably enough to be witnessed by thousands. In the 1870s a series of curious Bigfoot-style reports came from the region just a bit southeast of Geneseo. In 1957 a large and curious burial mound was excavated on the banks of the Genesee in this area. It was the work of a culture thought to have predated the Hopewell, which would be going wayyyyy back. I've written about this area from many perspectives, most of which you can access in other parts of this book. I bid you note it as a region of mystery out of all proportion to its size.

8) An arc south and west brings you to Allegany County's North Valley (north of Centerville, south of Eagle and Bliss), once home to a Native American nation that just disappeared. They and their former valley are known only as **Lost Nation**. What would you call them? No one knows their language, their culture, even their names for themselves, much less what happened to them. The Lost Nation may have been caught in the Iroquois Confederacy's seventeenth-century struggle with the Huron and Algonquin over the fur trade; but an extinction this total would be evident to archaeology, and we're out of ideas. I'm not ready to speculate about mass UFO abductions; but no tribe that could have been the Lost Nation is mentioned in the 1794 Canandaigua Treaty. They just vanished. Their valley has been a zone of mystery since, including outbreaks of critter-sightings. One in the late-1960s was merely suggestive: overnight pranks with farm equipment, some displaying titanic strength. Other incidents were more threatening, such as German shepherds and cattle being cowed by something in the trees. One cluster of sightings in the mid-1970s raised a mighty flap.

9) Once the **Cassadaga** Swamps were formidable. In 1828 a lost local named Jonathan Bugbee had to rely upon the guidance of a mysterious light in the low sky - something that

tHe X-pLaCes

could only have been a UFO - to guide him to safety. This was a report spectacular enough to have made Charles Fort's survey of world-mysteries. Ancient mystery seems to be here as well. Earthworks found here may point to the area as a shrine, maybe even a "City of the Dead," to many Native American societies. Several old writers have mentioned the burial mound that was excavated here and gave forth at least one very large human skeleton. The ancient graded road found along the lake is a curiosity at the least, since no one known to accepted history could have accounted for it. Several classic Bigfoot reports come from this area. In 1907 a hunter observed a massive humanlike ape. In another incident (reckoned from the memoirs of a local to have occurred in the 1920s) a hunter tracked giant humanlike footprints for miles through the swamp. Today we have the lovely Spiritualist community of Lily Dale and a trio of lakes tame enough to swim across. There has to be some residual energy about the place that attracted Lily Dale, the American Spiritualist "capital."

10) There's talk of a **Dead Zone** in a wooded area about two miles from **Mayville** in Chautauqua County. It's a patch of woods a miles or so square, probably a mile and a half from Dinsbier Road, in which the vegetation seems off: tangled, denser, forbidding. The very tone of the natural world seems altered, as if some mysterious occult force controlled it. It sounds like a mini-Mirkwood. For one thing, it's so tangled as to be nearly impenetrable. Living deer won't run into it, preferring to face the hunters and be shot. Wounded deer who struggle into it as a last resort can't be found, even at the end of a blood-trail, as if something snatches them up. Strange lights are reported in the depth of this area, from which the natural sounds of the wood can't be heard. Even the crickets don't chirp.

You'll want to clear that last stop as fast as you can. If your momentum scoots you over Lake Erie, wave to "South Bay Bessie," the gigantic serpent so often reported hereabouts. Keep an eye peeled for phantom ships, and particularly the lake's most noxious bogie, a sufferin' spaniel called "The Black Dog of Lake Erie." I don't suppose it will bother you much on your UFO, but it's best to be cautious as you enter the "the Great Lakes Triangle," a pattern of disaster far more lethal and significant than Bermuda's more famous trilateral.

B
The Power Points

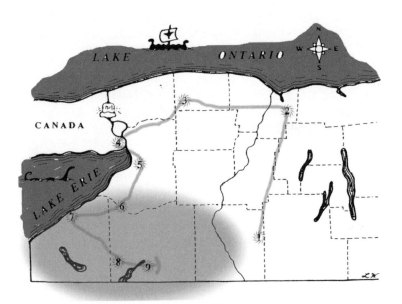

"The Force," we call it, fully intending to evoke *Star Wars*. One reason the films resonate for so many is the fact that they echo at least the outlines of ancient mysticism, one of whose fundamentals is the sense of an indescribable energy that runs through all things, that humans can channel into psychic abilities, that has high points in the earth, and that shows itself as a sense of the sacred - almost always an inspiring positive - and in the sprouting of psychic lore of all types, which to many people is a scary negative. We all acknowledge that the nature and the very presence of this force is debatable. There can be a time for that debate. Here's where we look at some Western New York spots at which this earthly energy is high, natural power-points the tradition of ages has recognized. These are places you can go and, feel the power.

1) They say the name *Kanakadea* means "where heaven and hell meet earth." Who knows what that was to the Iroquois? Age-old suspicion and a new cloud of folklore attach to the Kanakadea Creek valley near **Alfred** in which SUNY Alfred and Alfred Tech are located. The **Valley of Madness** held many aboriginal earthworks, but other supposed explana-

tions for the weirdness - ancient battlefields, Colonial massacres, and Iroquois burial ground - are either unverifiable or false. There's no denying the eerie folklore. Hunters and hikers experience strange sounds at twilight, strange "things" in the trees at dawn and dusk, and strange images at the eye-corners all the day. After dark some say you can hear drumming and see spectral Native American figures bearing their dead. Others report Revolution-era ghosts, possibly images from Sullivan's Campaign against the Iroquois. Passing through this valley is "The Forbidden Trail," an ancient wartime shortcut path over which Seneca war parties sped to strike into their foes' territory. Its existence was kept secret, its use was forbidden to all but warriors, and the penalty for transgressing was deadly. Twentieth-century hikers have reported ominous visions all over this trail, but it's a long one, and it merely passes through this "Valley of Heaven and Hell." Whatever the source, something has given this region an energy that makes people say they see things.

2) Where Lower Fishers Road ends at Log Cabin Road in **Victor** was a curious point of power. It started in 1855 on the day after Imbolc (the Celtic high holy day of February 1). Charles Fisher bought the farm in between some land he already owned. In the process of turning it all into one big spread he cleared four acres of old-growth forest and exposed a rich muck that at night gave off a phosphorescent glow. Maybe there's a scientific explanation for this; but the off-the-boat Irish moving into the area to work on the railroad were mightily impressed. At home they were accustomed to the surreal evening gleam of the peat bogs; that and the fireflies had become involved with the lore of the fairies, serious business to many of them. Talk of the Little People started up in all its ramifications at the **Fairy Farm**. A glacial boulder that looked like a human head was in the path of the road being built near Irondequoit Creek. As it was obviously sacred to the fairies of the region, the Irish laborers charged with moving it refused. Quite a beef started over the matter. The stone was taken several times, only to reappear the next morning in its usual place. One night it just disappeared, with no explanations. Instances of prophecy were associated with people who lived on this farm, which seemed only "true-telling," another fairy gift. Many fireflies and "fairy rings" - circles of discoloration associated with the Little People's dancing - were found here. When Homer Hill want-

ed to build a race track on the controversial field, his superstitious wife threw herself in front of the graders. The Hills never lost their suspicion that their differently-abled daughter Mae was a *changeling*, in Celtic folklore a defective fairy substitute for a human baby. (Today's Iroquois use the term to mean something different.) The Hills aren't here any more, but you can get a look at the region and maybe sense a bit of its glow. And remember that one of the most active traditions among the Iroquois is that of the Little People.

3) In July 1991, a crop circle twenty feet in diameter was found on the Roberts family farm in **Medina** by the corner of Salt Works and Maple Ridge roads. Its stalks were flattened and whirled into a circle, "a finely-woven fan-like pattern," reported Daryl Hardes, who studied it before the mobs arrived. The stalks had grown with a 90-degree bend, and soil taken from the circle was 100% sterile. (Many circles have been hoaxed, but you couldn't have done this one with ropes and boards.) Hardes found a second circle in a nearby cornfield, and Shane Sia noted four more nearby the same week not far from Culvert Road. The original circle was a visible discoloration until the snow fell. A few years after the circle on her property, Mrs. Roberts witnessed a queer, dust-and-wind affair like an earthy water-spout cross her yard. This might back the theory that some crop circles are caused by weather effects like tornado touchdowns. Many of the world's crop circles come with UFO reports; strange lights in the air were spotted the night before the Medina circle was found, and across the road from it lived someone who'd seen a UFO at another time. While these may be literal UFOs, I go back to the phenomenon Paul Devereux has popularized as "earth lights," and wonder if the energy of the earth isn't behind the Medina circle from the get-go. I think this is an energy-point which was observed during an energy-week.

4) Ontario's **Point Abino** is a limestone promontory forging a mile and a half into Lake Erie. Its dunes seem mountainous, and in back of them are marshes, meadows, and sandy tracts. One of the last in the private Point community holds a shrine-like natural space called **The Garden of the Gods**. Some great Architect must have crafted the central formation, a natural ring of trees and other vegetation. The accesses to it are private, but if you get close with the locals "in the know" you might be able to find this Garden of the Gods,

tHe X-pLaCes

about twenty miles south of Niagara Falls and twelve or so west of Buffalo. Our name for this pastoral mandala of trees and foliage may be only a century old, and who knows what the Native Americans called it before that? But they knew of it. The chert here - glassy rock, ideal for tools and projectile-points - was mined and traded across the continent for at least ten thousand years. To generations of American summer-settlers its sanctity was proverbial. But now it's hard to spot, even for the experts. In 1988 a historian and a naturalist familiar with the area made a pilgrimage to the Garden of the Gods. A short walk along the Sandhill Trail through a deciduous forest brought them to the special spot which was even then almost unrecognizable. The big ice storm of 1969 and some slovenly 1980s neighbors had pretty much destroyed a site whose harmony and natural *feng-shui* may have lasted millennia. Surely the energy that made it is here, if you could find the exact spot and stand there long enough.

5) Private, atmospheric Shale Creek Gorge is layered with energy and tradition. In daylight the namesake of **Eternal Flame Falls** in **Orchard Park** is virtually invisible; at night its three- to nine-inch-long natural gas jets make a spectral campfire behind the faint waterfall, a light as ghostly as any that appears in mythology or folklore. Winter's ice and Spring's floods extinguish the flame, and hikers light it again. Many contemporary visitors believe that if they listen hard enough on the right nights, they can hear the sounds of the ancients - chanting, drumming, humming - in the natural noises of the site. Others get so entranced that they even see them, shadowy images of stalking and dancing figures that come to life like holograms in the eerie glow. Shale Creek Preserve is just a hundred or so yards off of Chestnut Ridge Road. Because of the shape of the gorge and the line of approach to the flame, Amy Reed considers the energy of this site female. Maybe so. This is a tender flame, and the moment of lighting it isn't dangerous; but the approach to it, and the departure, may be all you're worth, so take precautions. (In this case, flashlights if you go at night, and good climbing shoes at any time.)

6) One of the most storied energy-spots in Western New York may be **Indian Hill** at the edge of the village of **Gowanda**. The road cutting over it to the Cattaraugus Reservation imitates the hill, gnarled, curving, and heavily wooded. The

many accidents on it may be due to its snaky nature, but nothing we know explains the legacy of folklore about it, a place "dragon-ridden," as Yeats would say. Anyone bold - or silly enough - to be here on certain nights may hear eerie sounds coming from the hollows holding old graves and homesteads. An apparition widely seen on the road is one they call "The Milkman" with no explanation. This is another Western New York zone of "witch lights," widely reported among the trees. The image of a wolf in a glow, sort of a sphere of dim light, has been reported. (This was almost surely some type of shaman in animal-guise. These are thought to be very dangerous.) Phantom people are also reported in the woods at twilight and around distant campfires, seldom distinct enough to be studied. I haven't heard even folkloric reasons for there to be so much psychic energy about this hill. Maybe it does come from some feature of the hill itself.

7) It's not common to find ghosts outside. I'd consider **Three Man Hill** a simple haunted site if people reported simple specific ghosts of it. As it is, it seems a big natural feature, the case of an outdoor energy-site by SUNY **Fredonia** that shows itself with a variety of psychic experiences. It's nicknamed for the three metal sculptures on it and sometimes called "Tin Man Hill." The spot is so active in local folklore that explanations have already been concocted, including "old Indian battleground." (It's not one of the ones Michael Bastine and his Seneca friends mention.) An ancient ring-fort was somewhere north of the first village (as this site is), and I wonder if that could be the explanation for the oddly circular depression at the heart of the wood on Three Man Hill. Two beautiful trees just behind the hill form a gateway into this small wood into which observers feel "invited" to walk. They feel inexplicably drained - or brightened - when they answer such a call. Many students come here at night to watch the stars and take in the sublime ambiance, and not all of them come away the happier for it. One October night so late it was early two people noticed that the wooded area looked unusually dark and still. They studied it, and noticed a gentle effect, a flurry of tiny lights that flocked from all directions and disappeared into the grove, which seemed to swell with light and return to its natural tone. But the mood of the hill can change. We all know the sense that some nights, dawns, or twilights have a little more charge. Shadows move on

tHe X-pLaCes

rooftops and dart through vacant grounds. ("The heebie-jee-bies," a friend at Lily Dale calls the feeling.) Maybe those aren't the right times to visit the hill. Once the sense of a voice ("GET OUT!") came to several people at once, "like a flash of words miles high in bold letters seared across my mind." On nights when the hill is restive, others report the sense of being followed by some radiating force that stilled treefuls of merry birds in its wake. They look back, almost envisioning it, dreading to confront it, dreading more that it might follow them to where they live. They face it until the birds start to sing again, even if it takes till full dawn. The hill seems to have its personalities, like one old woman who approaches students, quizzes them, then floats or demateri-alizes away.

8) By the mid-1800s Euroamerican mystical circles thought of Western New York as a center of "the earth-force," maybe connected with the young study of electricity, then supposed an almost mystical thing. The force was thought especially strong around **Randolph**, making the area conducive to all forms of psychic/spiritual communication. That could figure. Randolph has a penchant for producing or attracting free-thinkers. (Among them was Frederick Larkin, "New Age" doctor, freelance archaeologist, and author of *Ancient Man in America* and a couple other imaginative histories. Remember the Randolph Eclectic Medical College, an alternative association that started in 1848.) The town of Randolph was built on a massive ancient earthwork and was flanked by numerous others. (Almost no traces of them are visible now.) The idea that Randolph would be a good place for a major psychic experiment made sense to the spiritual-ist-inspired Kiantone community of John Murray Spear. Spear had a predilection for spirit-guidance, and in one of his trances came directions for a perpetual-motion machine powered by "the magnetic life of Nature." In 1853 they set about making the "Physical Savior," only one of its many names. "At precisely the time designated," Spear wrote, "motion appeared, corresponding with embryotic life." The critter was cared for like a newborn in the mid-town barn of wealthy supporter Thaddeus Sheldon (1818-1868), probably on the site of today's Sammy's Diner by the longtime Randolph Inn. But word spread in Randolph and a mob beat the zinc out of the fiendish machine, burning the barn in the process. Spear's guides in this venture were consoling when

next they spoke, proposing "a universal method of conveying thought," and, toward that purpose, "a central telegraphic station" on a Randolph hill christened "Highrock Tower." The spooks forgot to mention the trick of building it, which would seem to be the most important part.

9) One of the most fabled stretches of territory in Western New York is a bit of flatland near **Salamanca** and the Allegany River through which the state routed its expressway. Author and storyteller Duce Bowen recalls this region as the scene of a battle between cultures that predated the Iroquois. Thousands of spirits here are still unsettled. The Seneca named this area **Witches' Walk** because it was so haunted that the only ones who dared cross it after dark were witches. Only at night was it so easy to know them, huffing red glows from their mouths and nostrils as if they had fires inside them, fanning fuller as they toiled along the trail named for them. Some "in-the-know" Whites talk of Witches' Walk guardedly, as if it needed protecting from pothunters, for Gods' sake! Many stories of witches and shapeshifters are set in this area. We'll focus on it as a natural mystery-place, a region of psychic folklore and experience whose energy should still be strong. It's near a bridge on the I-86 just east of the Quaker Road exit, near a boat landing. The tracks used to go through here, and even the railroad wasn't safe from its magic. One night the train met some obstruction, possibly something someone saw on the track. A conductor got off to check on things. He never got back on. Maybe you'd be best advised to hang out on the bridge at the Quaker Road exit and just gaze into the trees to the north of it. And make tracks if you see any of those lights.

10) Early in the 1990s a group of spiritual friends started meeting, a handful from Rochester, the rest from Erie County. You could probably call the twenty regulars neo-Spiritualists, attached to no church or religion, inspired by their impressions of Native American spirituality and the new occultism of landscape. With the idea of "simulacra" - natural features that, from high above, look like something symbolic of an earthly spot's oldest name - a pair of lady psychics went into trance, came up with the vision of a vast, perfect, green pyramid under a Southern Tier hill, and became leaders of what I call **The Quest of the Holy Shale**. A metaphysical beacon, an inter-dimensional vortex, and a rendezvous site for UFOs,

tHe X-pLaCes

this giant crystal was thought to be the source of the mighty, radiating influence that drives the spiritual activity in our region. A lot of human energy went into the attempts to find it. On the counsel of the spirits, the questers formed motorcades through the Western New York and Northwestern Pennsylvania landscape. ("New Age joyrides" huffed a friend of these wagon-trains that often lasted days.) Now and then one of the psychics would call a halt, sniff the spiritual "vibes," and head them all in a new direction for the mystic hill. They may have named themselves "Emerald." Weary with the search (and the rivalry of the leaders), the group lost critical mass, and then the energy to sustain itself. The failure of the sacred mountain ever to turn up could not have helped. How they'd have known it should it even exist, this perfect green, lucent pyramid hundreds of feet high, beneath hundreds more of mountain, is another question. I wish I could tell you where, or even if, it is. Like the force that may have driven the search for it, I think it only shows itself in its signs. Make no mistake, though, I've been told: these women had power. ("It was alarming to feel yourself so... probed," said one of the people they "interviewed.") And psychics whose integrity I respect claim that there is something analogous to what they were seeking beneath one of the hills of our region, and that several times they were close to it, though they never knew. I'm putting a smudge on the map where, as best I can figure, the group did most of its looking, in a zone we already know as one of mystery. After all, half our power-point tour has been here. Feel free to drive in these hills and envision it. And let us know if you find it. You can call collect.

CREDITS

It's impossible to credit everyone, but those who have helped compile information include all those mentioned in my earlier books and:

Christina Abt	Dr. David Flanagan	Brian Nagel
Amy Alden	GHRS.org	Christopher Newton
Chris Andrle	Paul Gromosiak	Pam Newton
Daniel J. Anzalone	Daniel Harms	Phil Palen
William Bowen	Rosemary Hayes	Marilyn Palmer
Karen Canning	Patricia Hixon	David W. Parish
Bob Caple	Sara Hood	Nancy Piatkowski
Janet Cecere	Fredric Isaman III	Betty Robbins
Dawn Close	Michael Johnson	Rick Rowe
Sue Conklin	Rachel Joy	Andy & Elizabeth Sachs
Tom Cook	Mary Ketter	Richard Schulte
Cheryl Delano	Julia Kittsley	Jennifer Sirgey
David Dickinson	John Koerner	Andrea Snyder
Jim Difiglia	Chuck LaChiusa	Pat Taylor
Melissa Dunlap	Mike & Sherry Lesner	Rich Tazkowski
Joelle Eddy	Sharon Lubitow	torontoghosts.org
Dr. Denise Emer	Linda & Leo Lubke	Dr. Libby Tucker
Mary Beth Fagan	Lynn Metzger	Kyle Upton
Don Fields	Lora Milburn	Dr. Carolyn Vacca
Dr. Lydia Fish	Melissa Kate Miller	Charles Wesley

Through their knowledge and their direct effort on behalf of this book, these people virtually co-authored certain sections:

Duce Bowen	Melissa Jacobs	Pete Sexton
Matthew Didier	Katherine Johnson	Shane Sia
Andy & Mindy Hoeh	Chris Kurtanik	Jeanne Taradena

SOURCES

This is a book of folklore and factoids. Thorough accreditation would be as long as the text. Attempting to credit folklore would be silly, and also hard. (A lot of people who talk to me about UFOs and ghosts don't want to be identified.) This book has been put together through interviews with many individuals. In other cases the sites themselves - colleges, inns, parks - provided basic information, much of it through interviews or their own websites or literature. Where not specified, literary sources should be presumed to be those used in putting together my own research books *Shadows of the Western Door* and *Spirits of the Great Hill*.

Almost all Rochester information comes from articles in the *Rochester Democrat & Chronicle*, from Shirley Cox Husted's *Valley of the Ghosts*, or from Sheldon Fisher's collections.

My understanding of the War of 1812 comes from articles by Chris Andrle, Cynthia Van Ness, Jerrod Rosman, and Austin Fox, and interviews with Matthew Didier.

I'm indebted to Chris Brown for most Allentown information.

Contact my website masonwinfield.com and I'll help you track down any of my sources.

Part I - A TOUR OF HAUNTS
1) Haunted Inns
Interviews: Globe Hotel, Lincoln Hill Inn, Angelica Inn
Brochures: Belhurst Castle
Shadows: Grand Island's Holiday Inn, Frontier House
Spirits: Villa Serendip, the Athenaeum, The White Inn, Dock at the Bay, The Lighthouse, The Angel Inn
2) Haunted Mansions
Interviews: The Coatsworth, the Gardeniere, The Mansion (Buffalo), the Folsom House, the Mills Mansion, the Spencer-Chandler Mansion, Appleton Hall
Shadows: The Pink House, the Octagon House, the Van Horn Mansion
Spirits: The Maytham Mansion, the Dolls' House
Lecture of May 17, 2000 by Pat Mahoney: Graycliff
3) College Spirit
Interviews: St. John Fisher, U of Rochester, Daemen
Shadowlands and Haunted New York at All About Ghosts websites: SUNY Brockport, Elmira College, Hobart & William Smith
Shadows: SUNY Fredonia, St. Bonaventure
Spirits: Niagara University

4) Grave Haunts
Shadowlands and Haunted New York websites: Gurnsey Hollow
Interviews: Gurnsey Hollow, Fish Hill, Buffum Street, Forest Lawn, Whitehaven
Shadows: Goodleberg, Old Main
Spirits: St. Patrick's, Ashford Hollow
Husted's *Valley of the Ghosts*: Mt. Hope, Holy Sepulchre

5) Holy Spirits
Interviews: Church of the Ascension, Tonawanda Baptist & Presbyterian
Haunted New York at All About Ghosts website: Amherst/Williamsville Synagogue
Shadows: The Basilica
Spirits: Holy Family Western Orthodox, Fourteen Holy Helpers
Husted's *Valley of the Ghosts*: Mother of Sorrows, First Spiritualist, Our Lady of Victory, Penfield Presbyterian

6) Battlefield Haunts
Interviews: Hampton's Corners, Flint Hill
Shadows: Fort Niagara
Spirits: Devil's Hole, Ganondagan
Chemung County histories: Sullivan's Hill
Louis C. Jones' *Things That Go Bump in the Night*: Sodus Bay
Article by Jerrod Rosman: The Torture Tree
Articles by Matthew Didier: Lundy's Lane, Fort Erie

7) Haunted Highways
Interviews: Sandhill, Black Nose Springs, Holland, Henrietta, & Delaware Roads; North Street
Shadows: Cold Spring Road, Interstate Route 90
Spirits: Spring Valley, Manitou Roads

8) Haunted Theaters
Interviews: Lucille Ball's, the Royal George, the Courthouse, Allendale theaters; Aurora Players Pavilion
Shadows: Sphere
Spirits: "the Reg"
Buffalo News Magazine article 10/26/80: Shea's

9) Haunted Landmarks
Interviews: Mt. Morris Dam, Six Flags Darien Lake, Allegany Reservoir, Buffalo Science Museum, Salt Mines, Vidler's, The Central Terminal
Spirits: City Hall, the Stadium
Interviews, town of Dansville's website: Macfadden's Castle

10) Spooky Communities
Interviews were done in all cases, and information was taken from *Shadows* and *Spirits*
Dennis W. Hauck's *Haunted Places*: Rochester

Part II - WAYS of the SPIRIT
A) Vision-Places:
Interviews: Indian Springs, Spirit Lake, Cold Spring, Burning Springs, Goat Island
Lyman's *Amazing Indeed*: Rock City
Spirits: The Circle-henge, the Great Hill, Spiritual Spring
Livingston County histories: Squakie Hill
B) Around Spirit Way
Interviews: Crystal Hill, Church of the Sacred Heart,
Shadows: New Jerusalem, the Mormons, Ararat, Basilica, the Ebenezers, Roycroft, the Brotherhood..., Harmonia,
Spirits: Lily Dale, Shiloh, Chautauqua, Oak Knoll, St. Bonaventure, Finney, the Fowlers, Millerism
Buffalo News article by Louise Continelli 11/4/2001: Fatima
Articles by Barry Shlachter (*Fort Worth Star-Telegram*/March 1999) and *Buffalo News* articles by Anthony Cardinale (4/11/99) and Richard E. Baldwin (4/7/98): Way of Truth Sect
Irene Beale, *Genesee Valley People 1743-1962* & Carl Carmer, *Listen to a Lonesome Drum*: The Covenanters

Part III - THE X-PLACES
A) The X-Zones
Interviews: The Dead Zone
Interviews, *Shadows*, *Spirits*: All other sites
B) The Power Points
Interviews: Indian Hill, Three-Man Hill
Shadows: Witches' Walk, Randolph
Spirits: Valley of Madness, Medina crop circle, Garden of the Gods, "Holy Shale"
Sheldon Fisher's *Fish-Horn Alarm*: The Fairy Farm
Bruce Kershner's *Secret Places*: Eternal Flame

THE ARTISTS
Front Cover: Thanks to Kitty Turgeon and the Roycroft Shops for use of the Dard Hunter print. Digital imaging by Christopher Janiga.
Title-page state map: Drawn by Kenneth Sheridan. Digital imaging by Christopher Janiga.
Maps: All site-maps are taken from a 1997 original drawn by Laura Wilder for *Shadows of the Western Door*. Digital imaging by Christopher Janiga.
Three Man Hill, page 119: Photo by Amy Reed.
Mason Winfield photo: Marc Dellas
Back Cover: Photo by Amy Reed. Digital imaging by Christopher Janiga.

The Contributors

Algonquin mystic and activist Michael Bastine speaks and teaches across the eastern states. A friend and confidant of the legendary Tuscarora medicine man Mad Bear, Mike continues Mad Bear's legacy of communication, preservation, and spiritual inclusiveness, all with the goal of a better world.

Artist, lecturer, actor, puppeteer, playwright, and "urban shaman" Franklin LaVoie is one of the treasures of Western New York. A teacher and student devoted to the ancient mysteries of the Niagara Frontier, Franklin is known for incorporating his philosophy and insights into unique stage designs and stunning puppet shows.

Born in East Aurora, Amy Reed spent 17 years in Los Angeles, working in television, music, and film. She has returned to Western New York, a California-licensed massage therapist, *feng-shui* consultant, and student of the old mysteries. Bringing a sense of rejuvenation and relaxation to any evironment is Amy's passion, since that's one climate in which spirit comes through. Amy's working on making that a reality for her fellow Western New Yorkers.

Mason Winfield (BA, MA) studied English and Classics at Denison University and British Literature at Boston College. He taught English for 13 years at The Gow School (South Wales, NY) and served as Department Chairman. Mason was ranked among the top ten Buffalo-area tennis players several times and won a 50K cross-country ski marathon. Mason travels widely and speaks on subjects of ghosts, Celtic and Iroquois supernatural folklore, and Roycroft occult tradition. His ghost walks of Buffalo, Allentown, and East Aurora have exposed thousands of people to the hidden traditions of our region.

Birth of a Publishing Company

The Buffalo area's most innovative publishing company will celebrate its 20th anniversary in 2004 by hitting a benchmark that few regional publishing houses achieve. By that time, Western New York Wares Inc. will have moved more than 175,000 books and other regional products into homes, schools and libraries around the world.

If all these books were laid cover-to-cover starting at the foot of Main Street near HSBC Center, the trail would stretch past the UB South Campus, snake through Williamsville, Clarence, Akron Falls Park and end somewhere around Batavia! Putting it a different way, we've printed and distributed about 21 million pages of information about our region. An impressive path for a company that sprouted its roots in trivial turf!

The year was 1984. The trivia craze was taking the nation by storm. Buffalo journalist Brian Meyer played a popular trivia game with friends in his North Buffalo living room, he envisioned a game that tests players' knowledge about people and events in their hometown. Western New York Trivia Quotient sold out its first edition in six weeks and established Meyer as an up-and-coming young entrepreneur.

A year later, he compiled a book of quotations that chronicled the feisty reign of Mayor Jimmy Griffin. Meyer refuses to disclose how many six-packs were consumed while sifting through hundreds of "Griffinisms."

A City Hall reporter for the *Buffalo News*, Meyer spent 15 years at WBEN Radio where he served as managing editor. As founder and president of Western New York Wares Inc., Meyer has collaborated with dozens of authors, artists and photographers. By 2003, the region's premier publisher of local books had published, marketed, or distributed more than 100 regional products.

A Buffalo native and graduate of Marquette University, St. Joseph's Collegiate Institute and Buffalo Public School #56, Meyer teaches communications courses at Buffalo State and Medaille Colleges and is treasurer of the Greater Buffalo Society of Professional Journalists' Scholarship Fund.

Meyer is assisted by Michele Ratzel, the company's business manager, and Tom Connolly, manager of marketing and distribution. The trio has nearly 45 years of cumulative experience in regional publishing. Connolly works as a news anchor and producer at WBEN Radio and co-authored *Hometown Heroes: Western New Yorkers in Desert Storm*. Ratzel works at the Park School of Buffalo.

Other Regional Books

Visit our Web site at www.Buffalobooks.com for a complete list of titles distributed by Western New York Wares Inc.

Shadows of the Western Door: Haunted Sites and Ancient Mysteries of Upstate New York – A supernatural safari across Western New York. Guided by the insights of modern research, author Mason Winfield pens a colorful, provocative and electrifying study of the paranormal.
ISBN: 1-829201-22-4 $13.95

Spirits of the Great Hill: More Haunted Sites and Ancient Mysteries of Upstate New York – Does a historic curse linger over the Niagara Frontier? Was Buffalo designed by occult societies? From Mark Twain's Buffalo ghost, to Houdini's Halloween, Mason Winfield pens a riveting sequel to his supernatural survey of the region.
ISBN: 1-879201-35-6 $13.95

A Ghosthunter's Journal: Tales of the Supernatural and the Strange in Upstate New York - A delightfully diverse smorgasbord of strange encounters, all of them set in Western New York. The 13 fictional stories are inspired by the files of Mason Winfield.
ISBN: 1-879201-29-1 $12.95

Buffalo Memories: Gone But Not Forgotten -- Blessed with a phenomenal memory, the late George Kunz began chronicling his recollections of his Depression upbringing. His anecdotes on everything from Bisons' games at Offermann Stadium to rides on the Canadiana and shopping excursions to 998 Broadway graced the pages of the Buffalo News. This book is a collection of about 200 of these anecdotes.
ISBN: 0-9671480-9-X $15.00

Victorian Buffalo: Images From the Buffalo and Erie County Public Library – Visit Buffalo as it looked in the 19th century through steel engravings, woodcuts, lithography and other forms of nonphotographic art. Author Cynthia VanNess has selected scenes that showcase everyday life and views of historic structures created by luminaries like Frank Lloyd Wright, Louis Sullivan and E.B. Green.
ISBN: 1-879201-30-5 $13.95

The Erie Canal: The Ditch That Opened a Nation -- Despite its shallow depth, the Erie Canal carries an amazing legacy. In canal towns like Lockport and Tonawanda the doors to the American frontier were unlocked. Written by Daniel T. Murphy, including dozens of photos.
ISBN: 1-879201-34-8 $8.95

Erie Canal Legacy: Architectural Treasures of the Empire State -- Photographer Andy Olenick and author Richard O. Reisem take readers on a 363-mile journey along the canal route. This hardcover book is comprised of full-color photos and an enlightening text.
ISBN: 0-9641706-6-3 $39.95

National Landmarks of Western New York: Famous People and Historic Places -- Gracious mansions and thundering waterfalls. Battleships and nostalgic fireboats. Power plants and Indian longhouses. Author Jan Sheridan researched nearly 30 National Historic Landmarks in the Buffalo-Niagara and Finger Lakes regions. Dozens of photographs, maps and an index.
ISBN: 1-879201-36-4 $9.95